Succeeding

at

Teaching

SECONDARY

Mathematics

*The authors wish to dedicate this book
to their children, Alan, Jack, Katie, and Sandra.*

Succeeding
at
Teaching
SECONDARY
Mathematics

Your First Year

Cheryl D. Roddick // Julie Sliva Spitzer

CORWIN

A SAGE Company

For information:

Corwin
A SAGE Company
2455 Teller Road
Thousand Oaks, California 91320
(800) 233-9936
Fax: (800) 417-2466
www.corwin.com

SAGE India Pvt. Ltd.
B 1/I 1 Mohan Cooperative
   Industrial Area
Mathura Road, New Delhi 110 044
India

SAGE Ltd.
1 Oliver's Yard
55 City Road
London EC1Y 1SP
United Kingdom

SAGE Asia-Pacific Pte. Ltd.
33 Pekin Street #02-01
Far East Square
Singapore 048763

Printed in the United States of America

Library of Congress Cataloging-in-Publication Data

Succeeding at teaching secondary mathematics: your first year / Cheryl D. Roddick and Julie Sliva Spitzer.
   p. cm.
Includes bibliographical references and index.
ISBN 978-1-4129-2763-5 (pbk.)
   1. Mathematics—Study and teaching (Secondary) I. Roddick, Cheryl D. II. Spitzer, Julie Sliva.

QA11.2.S87 2010
510.71′2—dc22   2009045333

This book is printed on acid-free paper.

10   11   12   13   14   10   9   8   7   6   5   4   3   2   1

Acquisitions Editor:	David Chao
Editorial Assistant:	Sarah Bartlett
Production Editor:	Cassandra Margaret Seibel
Copy Editor:	Cate Huisman
Typesetter:	C&M Digitals (P) Ltd.
Proofreader:	Susan Schon
Indexer:	Gloria Tierney
Cover Designer:	Karine Hovsepian

Contents

Acknowledgments

Corwin gratefully acknowledges the contributions of the following individuals:

Mary Kollmeyer, Mathematics Teacher
Lejeune High School
Camp Lejeune, NC

Amanda McKee, Mathematics Instructor
Johnsonville High School/Florence County #5
Johnsonville, SC

Melissa Miller, Middle Level Educator
Lynch Middle School
Farmington, AR

Gerald R. Rising, Distinguished Professor Emeritus
University at Buffalo, State University of New York
Buffalo, NY

Judith A. Rogers, K–5 Mathematics Specialist
Tucson Unified School District
Tucson, AZ

About the Authors

Cheryl D. Roddick is an associate professor in the Department of Mathematics at San José State University. She currently teaches mathematics and mathematics methods courses to preservice teachers in elementary and secondary education. She also supervises field experiences for student teachers at the secondary level.

Dr. Roddick's research interests include the conceptual understanding of fractions and how teachers' thoughts evolve relative to teaching mathematics. She has presented her research in local as well as national mathematics education conferences. She also facilitates K–12 inservice activities with teachers in local school districts. Dr. Roddick may be reached at roddick@math.sjsu.edu.

Julie Sliva Spitzer brings to this topic a rich background in mathematics, technology, and special education. As an associate professor of mathematics education at San José State University, she teaches methods of mathematics instruction to aspiring educators and supervises their field experiences. Dr. Spitzer continues to enjoy inservice work with teachers Grades K–12.

Her research interests include studying teacher and student attitudes toward teaching and learning mathematics, and best practices for teaching mathematics to special needs learners. She is a frequent presenter at annual meetings of the National Council of Teachers of Mathematics and at other local conferences. Dr. Spitzer can be reached at sliva@math.sjsu.edu.

Introduction

Throughout our collective years as mathematics educators, we have found that new teachers are concerned about many of the same issues surrounding mathematics education. We realized that there is a critical need to ease the transition to teaching mathematics, and it goes beyond the teacher preparation programs that new teachers have completed. Our goal with this book is to supplement what new teachers of mathematics have already learned about teaching mathematics and to focus on the key elements of successful teaching.

In this book we have used a combination of research, personal experiences, and observations of other mathematics teachers. We present all the ideas that we have found to be extremely important to the developing teacher of mathematics. We have included many of the common problems and big ideas in mathematics in many vignettes sprinkled throughout the book. The vignettes were inspired by real teachers in real classrooms, and we hope they encourage thought-provoking discussion on important issues in content as well as pedagogy in mathematics lessons for Grades 6–12.

We would like you to keep in mind as you read this book that there is no one right way to approach teaching and that you are already in the process of developing your own philosophy of teaching and learning. This book is meant to be used as a tool to help you think about the important issues that can shape the kind of teacher you are meant to be. We hope that by reading this book you will get a better understanding of the strong connections inherent in mathematics as a body of knowledge and begin to see how everything you teach can be connected to other concepts or understanding.

HOW THE BOOK IS ORGANIZED

Chapter 1: "A Glimpse at Mathematics Instruction." This chapter provides a look at mathematics instruction in two classrooms. With two vignettes we set the stage for the rest of the book by introducing elements of successful mathematics instruction.

Chapter 2: "Standards-Based Teaching." In this chapter we build on the elements of successful mathematics instruction from Chapter 1 by discussing standards-based teaching in mathematics. We look at the standards set forth by the National Council of Teachers of Mathematics, as well as discuss the importance of standards created at the state and district levels. We also provide examples of standards-based teaching relative to algebraic reasoning.

Chapter 3: "Engaging Students in Learning Mathematics." In this chapter we take a look at the three interrelated components of engagement: the affective, behavioral, and cognitive. We begin with the affective component in light of Glasser's categorization of a human being's five basic needs: (1) survival, (2) love and belonging, (3) fun, (4) freedom, and (5) power. We describe how each of these basic needs is reflected in the classroom and how you can use knowledge of these basic needs to create an inclusive classroom environment.

Chapter 4: "Engagement Strategies for Special Populations." This section of the book takes an in-depth view of strategies for engaging several special populations: special needs students, gifted students, and English language learners. We discuss strategies for engagement that are specific to these special populations. We then present an engaging activity involving permutations and discuss how this activity may engage special populations of students.

Chapter 5: "Assessment." This book would be incomplete if it did not address assessment and its importance in the instructional process. We look at the purposes of assessment, and we discuss different means of assessing mathematical understanding and give examples of each. We also discuss the backward design model for assessment and present suggestions for assessing special needs students.

Chapter 6: "Putting It All Together." In this last chapter, we discuss ways for you to incorporate the strategies in this book throughout your mathematics curriculum. We suggest ways to connect big ideas within mathematics as well as present ideas for you to connect mathematics across the grades.

Your first few years of teaching mathematics are a very exciting time. Whether you are a new teacher or simply want to take a fresh look at teaching mathematics, we hope that this book will provide you with a structure to plan and guide you through your teaching. We wish you the very best for a long and rewarding career.

1 A Glimpse at Mathematics Instruction

In this chapter we will discuss the following:

❖ An Algebra Classroom Vignette

❖ A Geometry Classroom Vignette

❖ Best Practices for Teaching Mathematics

The teacher walks into class and sees 28 faces staring back at him, all sitting in rows, one behind another. The room is barren except for the chalkboards on three sides and a few books on the teacher's desk. Today, like every other day, the teacher asks if there are questions from the previous night's homework. If there are questions about a particular problem, he works through the problem on the chalkboard and moves on to the next one. Following this daily routine, the teacher takes out his book, turns to the next section in the text, and lectures as he writes notes and works examples on the board. Rarely does he turn around and even look at the students, much less ask them if they understand his lecture. Finally, after he has completed three examples on the chalkboard, he writes the following assignment on the board: "problems 1–45 on p. 17; quiz on sections 6.1–6.5 on Friday." He then sits at his desk as the students work quietly on their homework until the bell rings to release them from class.

Does this scenario seem familiar to you? How did you feel learning math this way when you were a student? Whether this has been your personal experience or not, you probably realize that there is more to teaching mathematics than what we have just described. New research and technology have brought into question many of the methods of the past, and progressive classrooms of today are quite different from the classroom described above. This book can help you prepare for the many aspects of teaching mathematics so that you will be able to make informed decisions on what to teach as well as how to teach it. We begin by taking a look at two classes with teachers well versed in the latest methodologies of teaching mathematics.

TWO ILLUSTRATIONS

The first class is having an Algebra I lesson on slope and proportional reasoning; the other a seventh grade lesson on surface area. Both teachers are experienced and demonstrate many exemplary practices in the teaching of mathematics. As you read, see if you can identify these teaching practices.

VIGNETTE 1: ALGEBRA I—SHAKE ACROSS AMERICA

It is 10:12 on a Thursday morning, and Mrs. Malloy is busy gathering materials for her 10:15 Algebra I class. As the students enter the room, they are randomly assigned to sit at one of the eight tables. Four students sit at each table, and each table is provided with the following materials: a tape measure, a stopwatch, and four copies of the assignment shown in Figure 1.1.

This activity involves a real-world problem-solving scenario in which students are asked to determine how long it will take for a handshake to travel from the east coast to the west coast of the United States. Students begin by collecting data on how long it takes a small group of students to shake hands. They then use both proportional and algebraic reasoning to estimate how long it would take to complete the handshake. This activity incorporates meaningful mathematics as well as several of the big ideas in middle school and high school mathematics. It was selected because it involves active data collection, a variety of approaches, and a range of acceptable answers. In fact, there is no one "real" answer, since such an answer would be different every time the event occurred. The most important part about this activity is the mathematical reasoning and methods used to get an answer, not the final answer itself. See Appendix A for sample data and solutions.

Figure 1.1   Shake Across America

This project should be completed in groups of three to four students. On a separate sheet of paper, please respond completely and clearly to the questions listed below.

Shake Across America!

Materials: tape measure, stopwatch

An environmental group is organizing a "handshake across America." The group plans to have people line up from New York to Los Angeles and pass a handshake from east to west.

Data Collection

1. Have several members of your group form a line. Count how many students are in the line and measure its length.

2. Start a handshake at one end of the line. Use a stopwatch to find out how long the handshake takes to reach the end of the line.

3. Repeat steps 1 and 2 for four different lengths of the line (e.g., 3, 6, 9, and 12 students). You will need to get together with another group or two.

Proportional Reasoning

4. Use your results to estimate the number of students per foot.

5. The road distance from Los Angeles to New York is 2,825 miles, or almost 15,000,000 feet. About how many people need to be in the line?

6. Now estimate both the speed of the handshake (feet per second) and the ratio of seconds per foot.

7. How long will it take to have the handshake go across America? Explain how you found your answer.

8. Explain how you can use proportions to solve this problem.

Algebraic Reasoning

9. Produce a scatter plot of the data you collected, with length as your independent variable and time as your dependent variable.

10. Determine the line that best fits your data.

11. How does the slope of your line relate to what you found in the proportional reasoning section?

12. In theory, what should the y-intercept be? Why?

13. Use your line of best fit to get an estimate of how long the handshake across America will take.

Source: Adapted from Charles, Dossey, Leinwand, Seeley, & Vonder Embse, 1998, p. 344.

Mrs. Malloy introduces the lesson by showing a YouTube video of a Hands Across America infomercial from the 1980s. There is a short discussion on the economic situation of the 1980s that prompted the Hands Across America event. (Amanda McKee, personal communication, December, 2008). Mrs. Malloy then directs the students toward the handout that has been passed out.

Students recognize this as a group activity, and questions originally center on the roles of each group member. Since they have done cooperative learning activities before and are familiar with the different roles that members of each group need to play, Mrs. Malloy allows her students to brainstorm as a class to come up with the roles of the group. The students come up with following roles: timer (individual who keeps time with the stopwatch), recorder (person who records the results), and reporter (student who reports the results).

Mrs. Malloy has anticipated other questions, so she has the students demonstrate as a class how to collect data for the activity. She has twelve students line up, and another student times the handshakes as three, six, nine, and twelve students shake hands. A recorder records the times as the handshakes are being completed. As the rest of the class observes this demonstration, they also begin to see a need for a "clapper," someone who would clap to keep the handshakes going at a consistent rate. They then begin the activity.

As the students begin working in their groups, some raise their hands. Mrs. Malloy walks around the room and hears similar versions of the same questions. After addressing the questions with one group and hearing the same questions from other groups, she decides to bring the class back together and have a class discussion about the questions "How far apart should we stand?" and "How fast should we shake our hands?" After several groups are given a chance to explain their viewpoints on the matters, the class concludes that as long as they are consistent within their own groups, it is not critical that each group make the same decisions.

The students proceed with the activity and complete the data collection section without any other questions. As they move into the proportional reasoning section of the activity, they once again have questions. In this section, students are asked to estimate the number of students per foot, the speed of the handshake (feet per second), and the ratio of seconds per foot. The two main questions that arise focus, first, on how to deal with the many ratios that can be created, and, second, what to do with the data for three, six, nine, and twelve students. Mrs. Malloy has intended for students to use the data for twelve students when solving proportions; she has asked them to collect data for three, six, and nine students so that they have data for the scatter plot and line of best fit in the algebraic reasoning section. Yet she does not tell them this directly, since she wants to encourage her students to think about how the data can be best used. As she circulates from group to group, she listens to students explain their reasoning and guides them with questions of her own if she realizes that they are off track.

In the final section of the activity, students are asked to use data to produce a scatter plot and line of best fit in order to predict how long it could take to complete the handshake across America. Since the use of technology is encouraged in Mrs. Malloy's class to develop understanding, students feel comfortable using it as they see fit. While some students choose to create their scatter plots using graph paper, others choose to use graphing calculators. As Mrs. Malloy walks around the room, she answers questions from the groups and comments on their work. She also notes that many of the groups are coming up with a variety of answers. At the end of class, she tells the students that they will continue this activity the next day and that groups will be asked to report their findings verbally to the class and prepare a write-up to turn in to her.

The next day, students spend the first half of the class period finishing up the activity and creating posters to present their results. Mrs. Malloy checks the progress of each group and works with individual groups who still have questions. Students are then chosen randomly by a roll of a die to determine the order in which they will make presentations. Mrs. Malloy asks a member of each group to present the group's poster. They are also allowed to bring another student from their group if they want assistance.

As the groups report their findings, it becomes very clear there is a wide range of answers from the class. After the second group presents, the students begin a discussion about how there could be such a difference in the "right" answers. Mrs. Malloy has carefully chosen this activity because of its open-ended problem-solving nature; she wants her students to recognize the importance of justifying their work and to realize that, in this problem, it is in justifying each step of the process that the answer is determined to be correct or incorrect. Much of the remaining class time focuses on the process through which each group made its findings. Some time at the end is reserved to discuss the similarities and differences of the proportional and algebraic reasoning approaches as well as to make explicit the connection between the ratio of seconds per foot in the proportional reasoning section and the slope of the line in the algebraic reasoning section.

DISCUSSION

In this section we will focus on the following points:

❖ Meaningful Mathematics
❖ Making Connections
❖ Teacher as Facilitator
❖ Communication
❖ Positive Classroom Culture
❖ Effective Instructional Strategies

Now that you have read the vignette, we want to steer you back to thinking about the exemplary practices employed in this lesson. First of all, we review this activity through the lens of meaningful mathematics. Shake Across America addressed many areas of important mathematics and encouraged students to make connections to other areas of mathematics. These considerations are very important to Mrs. Malloy, since she works hard to teach all of the standards required by her district and state, and she often feels pressed for time to accomplish everything. With activities such as Shake Across America, she is able to pull together several concepts in a single lesson. You may have noticed that students investigated the same problem scenario using both proportional reasoning and algebraic reasoning, which helps to make explicit the connection between the ratio of seconds per foot and the slope of the regression line. Numerical and graphical representations were used, as were symbolic representations when finding the line of best fit. Students analyzed the data collected and used their regression line to help them predict how long the handshake will take to complete. Using all of these concepts in a single lesson helped students to construct links between mathematical understandings.

Beyond the specific mathematical concepts and connections, there were several teaching practices employed that are worthy of note. We continue the discussion of this activity by addressing these practices next.

You may also have noticed the stark contrast between the role of lecture in Mrs. Malloy's classroom and in the classroom scenario at the beginning of this chapter. Mrs. Malloy did not spend the majority of class time lecturing to her class. In fact, she was much more of a facilitator than a lecturer. Although Mrs. Malloy does lecture at times, she is conscious about the time she spends at the board in front of the class. She wants to make sure that students are given plenty of time to explore new material, to create their own understandings, and to connect new understandings to existing knowledge.

The facilitation of understanding played out throughout the activity as Mrs. Malloy guided her students. In the vignette you observed students asking questions about the assignment, yet Mrs. Malloy did not directly answer the questions. Instead, she gave her students opportunities to think about their questions, come up with responses, and defend their thinking. Mrs. Malloy believes exploration to be a valuable experience, and, in her opinion, lecture does not afford students enough opportunities to develop their mathematical reasoning skills.

Cooperative learning and communication are important components that accompany the philosophy of teacher as facilitator. After all, if the teacher is not going to give the answers, how are the students going to develop understanding? While Mrs. Malloy did not simply dispense all her knowledge to her students, she allowed for plenty of discussion, both in small groups and the whole class, so that students could help each other to make sense of the mathematics in the activity. In more than one instance, students arrived at conclusions without her direct instruction, and student discourse had actually facilitated the conclusions.

Mrs. Malloy was also consciously developing a positive classroom culture, conducive to enabling all students to learn important mathematics. She did this in many ways. First of all, she selected an activity that students could relate to. It was her hope that her students would be engaged in Shake Across America, would enjoy learning mathematics because of this activity, and would feel better about themselves as learners as a result.

Next, Mrs. Malloy used many strategies to include all learners and to promote equity in her classroom. She grouped her students; she does this so that everyone can experience working with different partners throughout the year. Students were also given different roles in the group so that all could participate and to lessen the likelihood of one person dominating the group. In addition, when students explained their group's work, they were allowed to bring a partner. This was done so that any student who might feel uncomfortable for any reason would have another student for support. Often, students who struggle with their English speaking skills or do not have confidence in their mathematical abilities will shy away from communicating with the large group and thus miss out on the important experience of communicating their thinking. Having a friend for support can help to alleviate some of their fears.

To further include all students, Mrs. Malloy utilized a variety of instructional strategies. In order to meet the diverse needs of students in her class, Mrs. Malloy thought in advance about the assignment and its prerequisite skills. A component of the differentiation process involves breaking down the concepts and

> This type of teaching does not occur without thoughtful preplanning!

skills and making them accessible to everyone in her class. For example, she anticipated students having some difficulty with how to begin the task, so she had the students model the activity; she also was available to provide support in areas such as determining proportions or lines of best fit when the students needed it. Mrs. Malloy provided the instruction that was needed to whoever needed it in an alternative way. She did not adapt the curriculum; she adapted her instruction to the curriculum. The following section describes some more possible adaptations for students.

ADAPTATIONS AND EXTENSIONS

This activity can be adapted and modified in a variety of ways and may be used with students in sixth through ninth grades or anyone taking Algebra I. Students could have the data provided for them, or they could collect data together as a whole class (rather than in small groups), similar to the way Mrs. Malloy had her students model it at the beginning of the lesson. When the entire class uses the same data set, the answers should end up being the same rather than spread across the wide range of acceptable answers arrived at by groups who collect their own data. (Note that if groups collect their own data, it more accurately represents the real life situation in that the answer will be different each time.)

Younger students who are not yet graphing linear functions can investigate the activity using proportional reasoning only. Conversely, this may be adapted as an algebraic investigation exclusively. Students could be directed to use either a high- or low-tech method of finding the line of best fit: graph paper, graphing calculators, or graphing software.

This activity may be modified to be more challenging and to include higher-order thinking. Students could be asked to determine when the handshake would have to begin on the east coast to end on the west coast at precisely midnight of December 31. Students could also be asked to make comparisons of the two methods: proportional reasoning and algebraic reasoning.

This activity could also be turned into a cross-curricular project with connections to social studies and economics. In Chapter 6 we explore this idea in more detail.

We now move on to the next example—surface area in the seventh grade.

VIGNETTE 2: SEVENTH GRADE— SURFACE AREA WITH POLYDRON SHAPES

Mr. Romo is preparing to teach surface area to his seventh grade class. This is his eighth year teaching seventh grade, and he has noticed similarities in his students' understandings from year to year. Most of his students remember the formulas for the area of basic two-dimensional shapes (rectangles and triangles). They experience difficulties with more complicated shapes, however, since they do not visualize how more complicated shapes, like trapezoids, can be created by combining basic shapes.

He has spent time earlier in the year using hands-on activities to give meaning to the area formulas for parallelograms and trapezoids based on rectangles and triangles. One lesson that he found especially valuable to his students involved using geoboards to create shapes. Students were able to use rubber bands to divide the new shapes into rectangles or triangles to find the total area. In his lessons on surface area, Mr. Romo plans to use a similar hands-on approach so that students can construct their own understanding of surface area. Students will use commercially available manipulatives called Polydron shapes to create different three-dimensional figures, and then they will take their figures apart to determine that the surface area is composed of familiar two-dimensional shapes.

Mr. Romo begins the activity by reviewing the area of two-dimensional figures. He asks his students to describe how to find the area of several figures that he has drawn on the board. He then begins to develop the concept of surface area of a three-dimensional object by talking about wrapping presents with wrapping paper. He introduces the Polydron shapes by showing six squares snapped together to form a flat "net" for a cube (see Figure 1.2). Students determine together that since the side length of the square is 1 unit, the surface area of the net is 6 square units. When Mr. Romo folds the sides up and snaps them together to form a 1 × 1 × 1 cube, students are satisfied that they can "see" that the surface area of the cube is still 6 square units (see Figure 1.3).

Once Mr. Romo has finished with his introduction to the activity, he divides students into groups and gives each group a packet of Polydron shapes (squares, rectangles, and triangles; hexagons could be used later for a challenge) and asks them to investigate the types of prisms that can be made with the two-dimensional pieces when they are snapped together. Students take about five minutes to put together various prisms and become familiar with the manipulatives. Each group of students is then directed to find the surface area of the different prisms they have created.

Figure 1.2 Polydron Net for a Cube

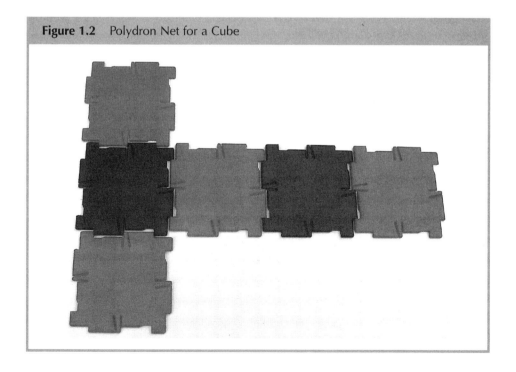

Figure 1.3 Polydron Cube Formed From Net

Students take about 30 minutes to find the surface area of their prisms. Mr. Romo brings the class back together for discussion and asks each group to tell the class what the surface area is for one of the figures they have assembled. When students are finished with their presentations, Mr. Romo asks the class to summarize their findings by giving a general description of how to find the surface area of a prism. This part of the lesson is difficult for many students, but he wants to give them opportunities to think about the patterns found in the prisms they have investigated. He encourages his class to give a verbal description of the formula for surface area as well as an algebraic description using variables to represent the dimensions of the sides of the prisms.

At the end of the period, Mr. Romo wants to lay the foundation for the lesson the following day. He plans to continue the investigation of surface area of prisms and challenge his students to make algebraic generalizations based on observed geometric patterns. He poses the following question for students to begin thinking about for the next day:

Given a square prism (a cube), how does the surface area of the prism change if each side dimension is doubled? Tripled? Quadrupled? Can you find any patterns in your answers?

The next day, students begin class by discussing this problem with their group members. They have lots of ideas about how to begin. One group decides to enlist the help of another group, and they each agree to create two different figures with the Polydron shapes and then share their created figures with each other. They quickly realize that while it is fairly straightforward to create a cube with six Polydron shapes that are one square unit each, and not too much harder to double the side dimensions, it is much more difficult to create shapes that are triple and quadruple the original side lengths, because the sides become much bigger and harder to work with (see Figure 1.4).

At this point a bit of frustration begins to set in. Mr. Romo observes this minor setback and resists the urge to help these two groups out. He has learned from prior experiences that students develop stronger understandings of mathematics when they work to figure out their difficulties without his help. He realizes, however, that there is a fine line between the right amount of frustration and too much frustration, which will lead his students to give up. And although he wants his students to construct their own learning, he does realize that some need a bit of help to get them to the next step.

Just as he begins to walk closer to the two groups, he overhears one student say, "This is too hard to put together! I am going to draw it instead." The student takes out a sheet of graph paper from his binder and draws the two-dimensional sides that make up the prism that they are investigating. He uses one square unit for the original side length, and then doubles, triples, and quadruples all the sides. Other students begin to follow his lead, and several chime in at once to help him figure out the new areas of each of the sides that make up the cubes. Since they have chosen to create square prisms with dimensions 1 × 1 × 1, 2 × 2 × 2, 3 × 3 × 3, and 4 × 4 × 4 units, their surface areas are 6, 24, 54, and 96 square units respectively.

They stare at their answers, and cannot come up with any patterns. Mr. Romo suggests to one group that they organize all of their findings in a table in order to

Figure 1.4　1 × 1 and 2 × 2 Units Created From Polydron Shapes

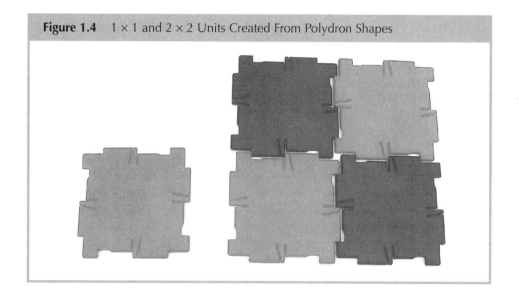

look for patterns. Since this strategy is one they have used in class successfully before, they are happy with this suggestion and begin creating the table. Another group spends some time looking at the nets they have drawn on paper, and these students notice that doubling each square produces an area that is bigger than the original area. Mr. Romo is happy that they have used their nets to help them find a pattern, and he encourages them to determine how much bigger the new area is than the original area.

By the end of class that day, most groups have come up with some patterns that they have found. Each group is given some time to share their findings with the class. Mr. Romo makes sure to ask each group to explain how they found their patterns, since some students created tables to help the patterns become more apparent, while others used the Polydron shapes or the nets they had drawn to help them compare the surface areas. One student was actually able to demonstrate his finding that when you double the dimensions, the surface area is four times the original area, and when you triple the dimensions, the surface area is nine times the original area. (See Appendix B for the table and algebraic generalization.)

DISCUSSION

In this section we will focus on the following points:

- ❖ Mathematical Connections
- ❖ Higher-Order Thinking Skills
- ❖ Facilitating Communication
- ❖ Engaging Learners in High-Quality Mathematics
- ❖ Adapting Instruction to Include All Learners

This vignette, like the first one, illustrates a lesson plan implemented by an experienced teacher, one who pays close attention to the many different factors that make up a successful learning experience. In this lesson, seventh grade students learned about surface area of prisms in a hands-on manner. Mr. Romo used his experience teaching the concepts of area and perimeter and extended it to measurement of three-dimensional figures. He was able to make mathematical connections come alive in a well-chosen activity that lent itself well to both algebraic and geometric investigation.

Notice that to set up the lesson for the second day, Mr. Romo posed a higher-order question to his class—that of determining the change in surface area when dimensions are increased. Students were asked to investigate this question and come up with patterns that they found. This question was given to the class to encourage deeper thinking about the concepts, yet it was posed generally enough to allow students to experience success at many different levels. This critical part of the lesson ensures that students are challenged beyond understanding of procedures and rules and are thinking more deeply about the concepts involved. Yet it is a component often overlooked by teachers who are simply trying to get through the text.

Communication was also a critical component. Plenty of small-group as well as whole-class discussion took place throughout the lesson. One of the great strengths of this activity lies in the rich discussions that took place during the group interactions. Notice that Mr. Romo did not spend the whole class period at the board doing all the work. Rather, he involved the students in their learning through active investigation and class discussion. Mr. Romo stepped back from the traditional role of teacher as lecturer and took on more of a facilitator role. He skillfully used classroom discourse to promote active learning by encouraging his students to reason through the questions themselves and construct their own understanding.

Mr. Romo's goal is to engage all of his learners in high quality mathematics, and therefore, he is always thinking of how to adapt or modify lessons to make them accessible to all of his students. Note that there were a variety of instructional methods used in order to include all of his learners, even those with special needs. English language learners' and special needs students' specific needs were addressed by using strategic groupings and multiple avenues to see the mathematics in different ways. He used various teaching techniques, such as active participation in solving problems, concrete and pictorial representations of surface area, and verbal discussion of the results. The first way he often introduces a concept is with a concrete representation. This lesson was no different; he used the Polydron manipulatives as a means for students to construct their own understanding of area and surface area. He is also aware of the importance of students verbalizing and clarifying their mathematical thinking in writing. This process benefits all learners, even students who may have learning difficulties or are learning English as a second language. Finally, he hopes that by engaging his students in activities such as this one, they will be more inclined to enjoy mathematics, have a positive attitude toward learning mathematics, and have more confidence in their own mathematical ability.

ADAPTATIONS AND EXTENSIONS

The use of Polydron shapes makes this activity engaging due to the hands-on nature of the manipulative. Polydron shapes are easy to snap together, so students can quickly create many three-dimensional objects for investigation. However, if Polydron shapes are not available, this activity can be adapted by using card stock or graph paper to create nets for the prisms that are being investigated. Students can fold up the nets and secure them with tape.

Students in Mr. Romo's class can continue to study surface area for several more days, investigating other shapes such as rectangular and triangular prisms, pyramids, and cylinders. Students who need a challenge could be asked to investigate more complicated shapes, such as hexagonal or octagonal prisms.

SUCCESS IN TEACHING MATHEMATICS

In these two examples, both Mrs. Malloy and Mr. Romo demonstrate commitment to high-quality mathematics instruction for their students. Many of the strategies they implemented have been identified by experts as best practices in teaching mathematics. On the basis of current research and beliefs on the teaching and learning of mathematics (Grouws & Cebulla, 2000; National Association for Gifted Children, 2005; Tucson Unified School District, n.d.; National Mathematics Advisory Panel, 2008), there is general consensus that the following statements are in line with best practices in teaching mathematics:

- ❖ Meaningful mathematics should be taught in a problem-solving environment that balances both conceptual and procedural understanding of mathematics.
- ❖ All students should be given the same opportunities to learn high-quality mathematics.
- ❖ Communication, both verbal and written, should be a means to facilitate students' reflection and clarification of their own understanding.
- ❖ Students should be engaged in constructing their own learning.
- ❖ Mathematics should be presented in a developmentally appropriate manner, using a variety of instructional methods and suitable support, such as technology and manipulatives.
- ❖ Assessment for both instruction and evaluation should be an integral part of instruction.
- ❖ Attention to beliefs and attitudes related to learning mathematics should be addressed throughout instruction.

SUMMARY

This chapter has provided a glimpse of what some of the many facets of successful teaching and learning of mathematics look like. The two examples describe classrooms in which teachers are flexible, listen carefully to their students, and adjust the discourse to support student progress and success. The importance of these features will be discussed in detail throughout the book so as to further support a new teacher's ability to master them in the classroom.

2 Standards-Based Teaching

In this chapter we will discuss the following:

❖ NCTM Principles and Standards for Teaching Mathematics

❖ NCTM Curriculum Focal Points

❖ The Singapore Bar Model

In Chapter 1, we presented two examples of teaching that provide insight into many successful methods used for teaching mathematics. The seven concluding statements on best practices were stated broadly, and several encompassed more than one idea. In this chapter we discuss standards to guide the content that you will teach in middle and secondary school. These standards contain valuable information on what mathematics to teach, how to teach it, and what principles should guide your teaching. It is no coincidence that many of the best practices highlighted in Chapter 1 are included in the standards as well. Those broad ideas are described in much more specific terms in the standards documents. In this chapter we revisit these useful practices and situate them within the documents that present standards for teaching mathematics. We also provide an example of standards-based teaching at the middle and secondary levels in order, again, to offer a clear picture of successful instruction that can be adapted for your own classroom success and that of your students.

WHY DO WE NEED STANDARDS FOR TEACHING MATHEMATICS?

Standards in any content area are designed to help establish what students should learn at each grade level or grade band. Standards typically stipulate the skills, concepts, and knowledge that are achievable. They should be used, in turn, to build criteria for assessments and establish goals for learning. Standards-based teaching is also an attempt to ensure that all students receive a high level of education in the area of mathematics. The National Council of Teachers of Mathematics (NCTM) has developed some guidelines to support this philosophy, and many states and districts have in turn created their own guidelines.

THE NATIONAL COUNCIL OF TEACHERS OF MATHEMATICS (NCTM) PRINCIPLES AND STANDARDS

In 1989, NCTM first published its recommendations for the teaching and learning of K–12 mathematics, called *Curriculum and Evaluation Standards for School Mathematics* (NCTM, 1989). The *Professional Standards for Teaching Mathematics* (NCTM, 1991) and the *Assessment Standards for School Mathematics* (NCTM, 1995) followed the initial document. These recommendations were subsequently revised to inform the current document, the *Principles and Standards for School Mathematics* (NCTM, 2000). This document presents six principles (equity, curriculum, teaching, learning, assessment, and technology) and ten standards (number and operations, algebra, geometry, measurement, data analysis and probability, problem solving, reasoning and proof, communication, connections, and representations), which make up a framework for a high-quality mathematics education.

Principles

The six principles represent an overall philosophy for teaching and learning mathematics:

- ❖ Equity. This principle supports the view that there should be high expectations and strong support for all students.
- ❖ Curriculum. The curriculum principle refers to having a cohesive curriculum that focuses on important mathematics, clearly articulated across the grades. The curriculum principle is very important, as it demonstrates the need to have all students learn important mathematics in a consistent manner. Before this document was written, the mathematics taught in U.S. schools varied widely, as there was no general consensus on what and how to teach.

Now, with these principles and standards, we have a clearer picture to guide teachers in the process of selecting the mathematics to be taught and methods to be used.

❖ Teaching. Effective teaching requires an understanding of what students know and need to know. It is also about using instructional strategies to encourage each student to reach his or her potential.

❖ Learning. It is important for teachers to use knowledge of their students, and of teaching and learning mathematics, in order to appropriately engage them in learning important mathematics. Learning should be built on students' prior understanding, and students should be active in their own learning.

❖ Assessment. Assessment should support the learning of meaningful mathematics and be informative for both the student and the teacher. More detail on assessment can be found in Chapter 5.

❖ Technology. Essential to teaching and learning mathematics is the use of technology. Technology can influence content as well as pedagogy and can enhance the learning process (NCTM, 2000).

Content and Process Standards

The ten standards are broken down into two groups, which speak to what to teach as well as how to teach it. Five mathematical content strands describe the content students should learn: number and operations, algebra, geometry, measurement, and data analysis and probability. Five mathematical processes highlight the ways of acquiring and using the content knowledge: problem solving, reasoning and proof, communication, connections, and representation.

The Five Content Standards

1. Number and Operations

This content standard encompasses the understanding of numbers and number systems. According to this standard, students should be knowledgeable about ways of representing numbers and the relationships among numbers, and they should understand the meaning of operations and how operations relate to one another. Students should also be able to compute fluently and make reasonable estimates.

2. Algebra

Algebra is an important topic that can be integrated across the grades, beginning in elementary school. Students should investigate patterns, relations, and functions. They should be able to represent and analyze mathematical situations and structures using algebraic symbols. They should use mathematical models to represent and understand quantitative relationships as well as analyze change in various contexts. At the end of this chapter, we describe a model for making sense of algebraic word problems.

3. Geometry

The NCTM standards state that geometry concepts need to be introduced at a young age and developed through middle and high school. Students should analyze characteristics and properties of two- and three-dimensional geometric shapes and develop mathematical arguments about geometric relationships. They should be able to use coordinate geometry and other representational systems to describe spatial relationships. They should apply transformations and use symmetry to analyze mathematical situations and use visualization, spatial reasoning, and geometric modeling to solve problems.

4. Measurement

Like geometry, exposure to and integration of measurement concepts throughout Grades K–12 are essential. Students should understand measurable attributes of objects and the units, systems, and processes of measurement. They should apply appropriate techniques, tools, and formulas to determine measurements.

5. Data Analysis and Probability

Students should formulate questions that can be addressed with data, and they should collect, organize, and display relevant data to answer them. They should be able to select and use appropriate statistical methods to analyze data as well as develop and evaluate inferences and predictions that are based on data. They should also understand and apply basic concepts of probability.

Content Standards in the Two Vignettes in Chapter 1

Looking back at the two vignettes in Chapter 1 and the manner in which the NCTM principles and standards were incorporated into the activities, it is worth noting that although the activities each address more than one content and process standard, not every lesson you teach will include all of the standards. In general, though, the richer the activity, the more content and process standards it likely addresses. It is important to strive to incorporate as many process standards as possible over the course of a unit.

The activities described in Chapter 1 actually address all five of the content standards, albeit to different degrees. In the Shake Across America vignette, students collected data to simulate people shaking hands from the east coast to the west coast. A small amount of data was collected, and the data was analyzed using ratios, proportions, and linear functions. Mathematical models were then used to predict how long it would take to actually shake hands across the entire span of the United States. The main two content standards covered coincide with the two different methods of analyzing the data: the use of ratios and proportions falls under the Number and Operations standard, while the use of linear functions falls under the Algebra standard. A third content standard, Data Analysis and Probability, is integrated into the collection and analysis of data through the use of lines of best fit to predict the amount of time a larger handshake would take. One could also argue that the Measurement standard is covered briefly when students measure time and distance while collecting the data.

The main content standard in the Surface Area With Polydron Shapes vignette is Geometry, with Algebra being a secondary content standard. Students use properties of geometry when building the different prisms and when investigating the surface area of the prisms. Algebraic reasoning is employed when students find patterns in the surface area related to the doubling and tripling of the side lengths.

The Five Process Standards

1. Problem Solving

Because problem solving can be challenging for students, it is important to provide multiple opportunities and to do so in a meaningful context. Students need frequent experience with solving problems in a variety of contexts. According to the NCTM (2000), students should be able to build new mathematical knowledge through problem solving. As students solve meaningful problems, they should solidify the mathematics they already know, extend their knowledge to include more mathematics, and develop fluency with skills. To help students bridge from existing to new knowledge, skillful teachers encourage students to apply and adapt a variety of appropriate strategies to solve a problem. In addition, students need to be provided with explicit strategies, such as Polya's four step process for problem solving (Polya, 1945) or STAR (Maccini & Hughes, 2000), also for problem solving. Polya's four-step process is as follows:

1. Understand the problem.

2. Devise a plan.

3. Carry out the plan.

4. Look back.

STAR is another first-letter mnemonic that is effective for general problem solving (Maccini & Hughes, 2000):

1. *Search* the word problem (i.e., read the problem carefully; write down the facts).

2. *Translate* the words into an equation in picture form (e.g., choose a variable, identify the operation, and represent the problem through manipulatives or pictures).

3. *Answer* the problem.

4. *Review* the solution (e.g., reread the problem; check for reasonableness of the answer).

In addition, students should also be given the opportunity to monitor and reflect on the process of mathematical problem solving.

The problems presented in the two vignettes are nonroutine problems, and as such, they require students to use their knowledge in different ways. Problem solving is used throughout the activities as the students apply a variety of appropriate strategies, such as collecting data, making three-dimensional figures, drawing pictures, and finding patterns to solve the problems.

2. Reasoning and Proof

Although it is important that students know how to solve mathematics problems, it is also critical that they understand why they are doing what they are doing. This process standard suggests that reasoning and proof are fundamental aspects of mathematics and that students should regularly investigate mathematical conjectures, evaluate mathematical arguments, and use a variety of methods of reasoning and proof.

In the Shake Across America activity, students were asked to solve the problem in two ways—using proportional reasoning and using linear functions. They used reasoning to predict from what was known to what had not been measured. As an extension, students could compare the two different approaches and make judgments on the reasonableness of their two answers.

One of the features of the Surface Area With Polydron Shapes vignette was the use of reasoning to determine what happens to surface area when the dimensions of each side are doubled or tripled. Students also used reasoning to develop methods to continue the pattern without actually building each of the prisms. They then constructed arguments to justify any generalizations of the patterns they found.

3. Communication

Understanding tends to be more complete when students are required to explain, elaborate on, or defend their position to others. Developing habits of verbalizing and writing mathematical examples and procedures can greatly help in removing obstacles to success in general mathematics settings. It is not always easy for students to communicate their personal understandings, but one of the most rewarding efforts a teacher can make is to begin early to help them to develop this skill. Throughout both examples in Chapter 1, students were fully involved in communicating their mathematical understanding. Communications allowed for expression in small-group discussions, whole-class discussions and presentations, and written form. In each of these lessons, students worked in groups.

4. Connections

Hiebert and Carpenter (1992) state that the degree of a student's understanding is determined by the number, accuracy, and strength of the connections he or she makes. Connections should be made and used within and among areas of mathematics as well as to other subject areas. As teachers grow in their experience, these connections will become more visible to them and can be reinforced for their students. Numerous connections were inherent in each of the two activities—connections within mathematical ideas as well as connections to the real world. The idea of ratio is connected to the concept of the slope of a line in the Shake Across America activity. The use of a mathematical model is connected to the solution of a real-world problem. Geometric and algebraic patterns were connected in the Surface Area With Polydron Shapes vignette.

5. Representation

"The ways in which mathematical ideas are represented is [sic] fundamental to how people can understand and use those ideas" (NCTM, 2000, p. 67). Using multiple representations involves communicating mathematics in different ways. Students learning mathematics often need multiple methods of viewing a concept in order to understand it. As students develop their understanding of mathematics, their repertoire of representations increases and becomes more varied. Students with special needs and English language learners can particularly benefit from use of multiple representations. (Chapter 4 addresses special needs students and English language learners.)

For example, in the Shake Across America activity, students used data in tables as well as symbolic and graphical representations of the handshake scenario. In the Surface Area activity, students used Polydron shapes as a concrete representation of the problem situation. Some students drew pictures, whereas others organized their findings in a table to look for patterns. All of these approaches involve different representations of the same problem situation.

These principles, content standards, and process standards offer a clear framework with which to guide your instruction. Greater detail is provided in the NCTM document itself. To read a full description, go to www.nctm.org or obtain *Principles and Standards for School Mathematics* written by NCTM (2000). The standards are divided into grade bands (PreK–2, 3–5, 6–8, and 9–12) and provide specific examples of how these standards look at each of the grade levels.

Many of the same ideas from the list of best practices in Chapter 1 are reflected in the NCTM standards just cited. It is important to mention again that these best practices, as well as the NCTM standards, are intended to guide you as you develop your curricula for all of your learners. The process of setting high standards for all students should include planning instruction based on the same age-appropriate curriculum and activities and does not mean that you teach a different set of objectives to part of your class. You should use the same goals and base curriculum for all of your students. Students who are lagging behind in basic skills or concepts should not use a different curriculum; they should just have opportunities to learn the curriculum in different ways.

In the coming chapters we discuss strategies that may be used to differentiate your instruction to include all learners yet still provide the same high-quality, standards-based instruction for your learners.

STATE AND DISTRICT STANDARDS FOR TEACHING MATHEMATICS

As mentioned earlier, most states have created their own sets of state standards, often written with the NCTM standards as guidelines. In addition, some school districts write their own standards, and these in turn are usually based on the respective state standards. Typically, the NCTM standards are more general than either state or district standards and written in multiple grade-level bands, whereas many state and district standards give specifics as to what skills and concepts should be taught at each grade level. For a new teacher of mathematics, it can be very confusing to sift through all of these documents. Yet it is important to familiarize yourself with them before your first day of class. Copies should be readily available to you online or from your principal, your mathematics department chair, or the mathematics curriculum specialist for your district.

THE RELATIONSHIP BETWEEN STANDARDS AND STANDARDS-BASED MATHEMATICS TEXTBOOKS

Many of the popular mathematics textbooks are now written to address current mathematics standards. These are often listed in the textbook or the supplemental material that accompanies the text. Although you may take great comfort in the thought that all the hard work of matching standards to curricula has been done for you, please be sure to read through the standards documents yourself, to be sure the standards are included in your text as intended by your school or district documents. Even though the textbook you are using may be standards based, it may not contain all of your grade-level standards, or it may contain higher or lower grade-level standards. You want to make sure your standards correlate with the textbook.

NCTM Curriculum Focal Points

If you find the idea of dozens of individual standards for mathematics at each grade level overwhelming, do not despair. Each standard does not have to be addressed in isolation, and many of them are written toward a common goal. In fact, there are a few key concepts that are critical at each grade level. Key concepts have been identified for Grades K–8 in the NCTM's *Curriculum Focal Points for Prekindergarten Through Grade 8 Mathematics* (2006). This document addresses the most important mathematics taught at each level and seeks unity among the different individual state documents regarding mathematics standards. For each grade level K–8, three curriculum focal points are given that consist of related knowledge, skills, and concepts.

For example, let's take a look at the three focal points for sixth through eighth grades:

Grade 6 Curriculum Focal Points

Number and Operations: Developing an understanding of and fluency with multiplication and division of fractions and decimals.

Number and Operations: Connecting ratio and rate to multiplication and division.

Algebra: Writing, interpreting, and using mathematical expressions and equations.

(Continued)

(Continued)

Grade 7 Curriculum Focal Points

Number and Operations, Algebra, and Geometry: Developing an understanding of and applying proportionality, including similarity.

Measurement, Geometry, and Algebra: Developing an understanding of and using formulas to determine surface areas and volumes of three-dimensional shapes.

Number and Operations and Algebra: Developing an understanding of operations on all rational numbers and solving linear equations.

Grade 8 Curriculum Focal Points

Algebra: Analyzing and representing linear functions and solving linear equations and systems of linear equations.

Geometry and Measurement: Analyzing two- and three-dimensional space and figures by using distance and angle.

Data Analysis, Number and Operations, and Algebra: Analyzing and summarizing data sets.

These focal points can help you to organize and prioritize the list of standards by providing a core set of topics at each grade level. They also give you an understanding of how big ideas, such as ratio, proportion, and slope, are integrated across several grades. At press time, the NCTM had not developed focal points for Grades 9–12; however, you may want to look at the big picture of each course you are teaching. You will probably be able to come up with several key ideas to focus on in each of the high school math courses as well. Although the focal points are not meant to be followed at the expense of other standards, they do help you to keep the most important topics front and center. These are the topics that need to be understood thoroughly for success in future study of mathematics.

ALIGNING ALGEBRAIC REASONING WITH THE PROCESS STANDARDS

When planning standards-based instruction, it is important to familiarize yourself with the standards for the courses before and after the one you are teaching in order to better understand the development of mathematical concepts across grades and courses. Such broader understanding enables you to build upon prior knowledge at an appropriate level for your students and to provide a proper foundation for future learning. This knowledge will also accumulate over time as you gain experience as a teacher and communicate with other math teachers.

One important content area that begins in elementary school and is developed across the grade levels is algebraic reasoning. Elementary students experience algebraic reasoning at developmentally appropriate levels, so that by the time most students reach middle school they have been informally introduced to basic algebraic concepts. At this point some students will be ready to study algebra more symbolically, while others will still rely on concrete or pictorial representations to further develop their understanding. Middle or secondary teachers can encourage their students' algebraic understandings by continuing to provide instruction in algebra using a variety of methods.

Jerome Bruner (1966), one of the best-known and most influential educational psychologists of the 20th century, noted that learners develop understanding of a concept by moving through three distinct modes of learning: (1) enactive, (2) iconic, and (3) symbolic. These terms could be translated as (1) using concrete manipulatives, (2) using pictures, and (3) using numbers or symbols.

When teaching a younger student, for example, you are most likely to teach concepts in a concrete, hands-on manner. Bruner advocated using manipulatives with younger students so that they can physically perform the actions represented by the mathematical symbols. Students would then progress to the pictorial stage, in which they would draw pictures of the actions instead of actually performing them. The final stage, the symbolic stage, involves the use of numbers and mathematical symbols to represent the quantities and actions implied by the pictures. These stages correspond to the process standard of Representation advocated by the NCTM. Additionally, research has found this progression (concrete, pictorial, and then symbolic) to be effective when teaching all learners, especially for special needs students and English language learners. When introducing new concepts, or reviewing previously taught concepts, incorporating concrete representations first is likely to engage more learners than the abstract-only approach. Although it is commonly assumed that high school students can operate at the purely symbolic level, many students of high school age can still benefit from this progression of representations.

Three Distinct Modes of Learning

1. Concrete—hands-on.

2. Pictorial—pictures.

3. Symbolic—numbers or symbols.

The Singapore Bar Model

Singapore is one country that consistently performs well in international tests of mathematics at various grade levels (Mullis et al., 2008). One of their approaches to developing algebraic thinking, the bar model, reflects Bruner's philosophy outlined above. All three of Bruner's stages—concrete, pictorial, and symbolic—are important, yet in typical middle and high school instruction in the United States, the emphasis is predominantly on the symbolic stage. Efforts are being made to incorporate more hands-on instruction, but the mode that is often lacking is the pictorial stage (Hogan & Forsten, 2007). The bar model is a pictorial approach that can be used to increase the use of such pictorial models in teaching mathematics. Let's look at how the bar model might be used when solving algebraic problems typically seen in middle and high school mathematics classes.

> Ashley is three times as old as Jessica. The sum of their ages is 24. How old is each girl?

This classic problem appears in algebra textbooks across the nation and is often solved symbolically using either one or two variables. We will look at the one-variable solution:

Let x = Jessica's age; let $3x$ = Ashley's age. The sum of their ages is 24, so $x + 3x = 24$. Solving this algebraic equation gives us $x = 6$, so Jessica is 6 years old and Ashley is 18 years old. As with many word problems, students can have trouble coming up with the value represented by the variable as well as the equation to solve. The bar model provides a visual to help students solve these types of problems.

Let one rectangle (bar) represent Jessica's age, and three bars represent Ashley's age as follows:

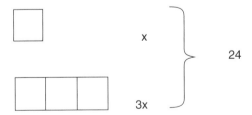

Since the sum of their ages is 24, the four bars altogether would represent 24. This visual can be used to help students set up the correct algebraic equation to solve. Or, it can be used to solve the problem without equations at all. The value of four bars equals 24, so the value of one bar can be found by dividing 24 by 4 to get 6. This means that each bar represents 6, and that three bars must equal 18. The beauty of this model is that algebra is just generalized arithmetic, and the operations used to solve the problem without algebra are the same operations used to solve the algebra equation.

This next problem is one that can be solved in Grades 6–8 using ratios and proportions:

> The ratio of Alan's allowance to Sandra's allowance is 3 to 5. Sandra's allowance is $120. How much of an increase in allowance will Alan need to receive to make the ratio of his allowance to Sandra's 5 to 6?

Without the bar model, one common way to solve this problem is by using proportions to solve for Alan's allowance for each given ratio. Let x = Alan's allowance, and set up the ratio Alan's allowance: Sandra's allowance. The proportion will then be $\frac{x}{120} = \frac{3}{5}$. Solving for x gives $72 for Alan's initial allowance. Setting up and solving the next proportion, $\frac{x}{120} = \frac{5}{6}$, gives you Alan's new allowance of $100. Subtracting $72 from $100 will give you the increase of $28 that Alan needs to have.

This multistep solution can be a bit overwhelming to some students, especially if they are not comfortable setting up and solving problems using proportions. Use of the bar model is one way to make this problem more accessible by providing a welcome visual. Let's look at how this problem can be solved with the bar model:

Since the original ratio of Alan's allowance to Sandra's allowance is 3 to 5, let's use three small bars to represent Alan's allowance and five small bars to represent Sandra's allowance:

Alan's allowance

Sandra's allowance

Since Sandra's allowance is $120 and it is broken up into five small bars, we can divide $120 by 5 to get $24, the amount represented by each small bar. Now we know that Alan's original allowance is $24 × 3 = $72.

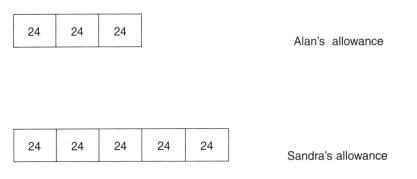

Now we need to know how much Alan's new allowance will be. Since Sandra's allowance does not change, we keep the total length of her bar the same. But now, since the new ratio is 5 to 6, we need to divide Sandra's bar into six equal parts, instead of the five original equal parts. Alan's allowance does change, so his total bar will be longer, and it will be five of the equal parts used to create Sandra's allowance.

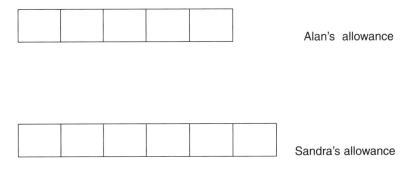

In order to determine the amount represented by one small bar, we need to divide $120 by 6 to get $20. Since Alan's allowance is represented by five small bars, his new allowance will be $20 × 5 = $100. Subtracting $72 from $100 will give us the amount of increase, which is $28.

You can see how the bar model was used in both of these problems to assist students in making the often difficult transition from concrete to abstract thinking. This method also serves to link prior understanding of arithmetic word problems to algebraic word problems. Younger students, or those who need additional assistance, can use blocks of equal size to solve the problems using a more hands-on approach. Algebra tiles would work well for problems of this type.

It is important to note that the pictures that are drawn represent the problem scenario and can be used to answer any number of questions from the given scenario, not just the specific question posed. This model has the added benefit that it can be used in elementary school just as easily as in middle or high school; teachers in elementary school can introduce the bar model to solve arithmetic word problems, providing a nice bridge to solving algebraic word problems later. This was demonstrated above in the age problem. In addition, students can "take" this model and use it anywhere, something they cannot do with concrete manipulatives. Finally, this model serves to address diverse learners in a class when purely abstract, symbolic methods are not accessible to every learner.

SUMMARY

In this chapter, we discussed essential information about standards-based teaching in mathematics and some examples of standards-based activities. We want to emphasize the importance of incorporating both the process standards and the content standards in your curricula. Traditionally, schools have focused on teaching the content via procedures and basic skills; however, equally important are the process standards that focus on critical thinking and problem solving, reasoning, communication, representations, and making connections to support learning. The two vignettes from Chapter 1 demonstrate the link between current research on best practices for teaching and the standards for teaching a subject, which should go hand in hand.

As you grow in your teaching, one of the best steps you can take is to increase your awareness of and attention to the process standards so that you may consciously incorporate them increasingly in your future teaching. These important standards are frequently overlooked in the teaching of mathematics.

3 Engaging Students in Learning Mathematics

Students are engaged when they are interested—challenged—satisfied—persistent—and committed to their school work.

—Center for Leadership in School Reform

In this chapter we will discuss the following:

❖ Engaging Learners
❖ Glasser's Five Basic Needs
❖ Affective Issues Related to Learning Mathematics

Over the next several years as a teacher, you will begin to develop your philosophy on classroom management. You have no doubt read about some of the many strategies of classroom management and have probably also begun to consider how these strategies fit in with your style of teaching. We would like to suggest in this chapter that the real issue is not management, but engagement—engagement with the topics that you teach and in the manner in which you teach them. If lessons are interesting, challenging, and meaningful and include all learners, students will be engaged in the learning process, and classroom disruptions can be minimized.

In the Chapter 1 vignettes, students are actively participating in their activities. New teachers will find, however, that such engagement must be nurtured and developed over time. Furthermore, there are issues specific to teaching and learning mathematics that can directly impact your students' abilities to engage in the tasks you set before them. These issues are reflective both of students' real mathematical abilities as well as their perceptions of those abilities and whether or not they themselves are an integral part of your classroom.

WHAT IS ENGAGEMENT?

According to Pintrich and Schrauben (1992), student engagement consists of three interrelated components: the affective, behavioral, and cognitive components. Affective factors include student interest in learning as well as the beliefs and emotions tied to their experiences in learning a particular subject. Behavioral factors include actions that can be observed, such as participation in a particular activity and communication with group members while solving a problem. Cognitive factors involve the mental effort and processing expended while learning something new. In line with this description of engagement, students who are sufficiently engaged in a mathematics lesson display positive emotions toward learning mathematics, actively participate in the activities of the day, and exhibit a dedication to thinking deeply about a given problem.

As we begin to discuss strategies within the three components of engagement, you may notice overlaps. These components are interrelated, and strategies for one often support the development of one or both of the others. For example, a teacher who uses strategies to develop a positive classroom culture (affective component) will also generally impact the students' participation (behavioral component), and thus the students' willingness to think about and learn a new concept (cognitive component). Promoting engagement in your classroom is no small feat, however. In this chapter we talk about these three interrelated components and provide insight into how you can encourage your students to be fully engaged in their learning.

ENGAGING LEARNERS IN THE AFFECTIVE DOMAIN

Let's consider some common scenarios when teaching mathematics.

VIGNETTE 1: MATH CLUBS

Mr. Herrera has plans to start a math club at the high school where he teaches. He fondly remembers the math competitions he was involved in as a student, and he would like to recreate that experience for his students. He becomes involved with the local math competition and develops a plan to prepare a team for the upcoming exam.

The initial response to his math club is overwhelming and surprising. Mr. Herrera had no idea that so many students were interested in learning about mathematics after school, in their spare time. At the first meeting, he encounters a sea of faces filled with anticipation, and, for a brief moment, he allows himself to dream about actually winning one of the math contests. He vows to work diligently to prepare the students for the first contest coming up in four months.

As the math club gets underway, attendance remains respectable, but it definitely drops off from the initial enthusiastic response. The contest preparation is going as well as can be expected, but Mr. Herrera has noticed that the practice test problems are quite challenging, and not as many students as he anticipated are able to solve them. When he starts to keep records, he notices that out of thirty problems on a sample test, the average number correct is eight. This concerns him a bit, but he tells himself that the students simply need more practice with the sample tests and that they will get the hang of it.

The day of the contest is filled with anticipation. Mr. Herrera's team of eight students has been chosen from the twelve students who regularly participated in the after-school math club. He is anxious to find out how they will perform.

But the events that play out that day are not what Mr. Herrera had expected at all. He learns that his students are up against a seemingly insurmountable challenge—that of competing with students from the top school districts in the county, many of which offer a special year-long problem-solving course in addition to their regular math course offerings. There are two parts to the competition: an individual exam consisting of thirty problems, and a team exam with eight problems. The top students in the county obtain perfect or near-perfect scores on both individual and team exams. In contrast, Mr. Herrera's students' individual test score average is eight out of thirty, the same as their average in all of the practice exams. At the end of the day, he congratulates his students on their good effort, but the disappointment felt by all is hard to conceal.

VIGNETTE 2: SEVENTH GRADE—MATH JEOPARDY

Mr. Hammond, a seventh grade teacher, likes to use games to help students review for mathematics tests. The game he has chosen today is based on the popular television show Jeopardy, *in which a clue is given and contestants have to come up with the answer. Higher point values are attached to the more difficult clues. In mathematics classes, students generally play the game in teams, and the first team to get the correct answer wins the advertised number of points. Mr. Hammond divides his class into teams and proceeds with the game. After a few rounds, it is apparent that Heriberto's group has taken a commanding lead, and the rest of the class begins to make comments to that effect. "Heriberto solves all the problems quicker than we can, Mr. Hammond. It's not fair!" Mr. Hammond continues without comment and finishes the game, but he wonders how effective it was in reviewing the important material from the chapter.*

These two examples are typical of scenarios played out by well-meaning teachers who are seeking to improve students' learning experiences in mathematics. Their intentions are noble, yet it is often the case that, even when teachers are aware that the experience is not quite what they intended, they are at a loss to make any improvements. The primary issue here is that of engagement: how to ensure that each student is participating in the learning process as fully as possible. This leads us to consider the general philosophy of Glasser's (1998) Five Basic Needs.

GLASSER'S FIVE BASIC NEEDS

A Description of Glasser's Five Basic Needs

A positive classroom environment is an essential component of teaching. The classroom climate that you create in the beginning of the school year will help to influence how comfortable your students will feel participating in your instructional activities. If the climate you have created is warm and welcoming, students will be more likely to try new experiences without fear of failure or ridicule. This is especially important in mathematics, in which many students have experienced failure and mathematics anxiety.

Glasser (1998) believes that all human beings have the same basic needs. He categorizes them into five categories: (1) survival, (2) love and belonging, (3) fun, (4) freedom, and (5) power. He also describes how each of these basic needs is reflected in the classroom.

The first need is the most basic: survival. This need encompasses everything necessary to live, such as food, water, shelter, and clothing. This basic need must be met before any learning can take place. Students who are struggling to survive will not be able to focus on school, much less on learning mathematics. If your students are coming to school hungry or sleepy, for example, it may be a sign that some of these basic needs are not being met. A teacher can seek to meet the other four basic needs in his or her mathematics classroom in simple, yet effective ways.

The need for love and belonging plays out in interesting ways in the mathematics classroom. Actively taking responsibility for one's own learning—by questioning, making mistakes, and trying again—involves a great deal of risk taking. Fostering such an atmosphere requires a sense of community between teacher and students, an environment in which everyone feels safe to investigate mathematics. Students who feel as if they "belong" in the classroom, who feel they are accepted for who they are and are considered valuable members of the community, are more likely to take risks in their learning and put forth effort in the classroom.

The sense of belonging a student feels in your classroom begins to develop on the first day of school and is affected by events both large and small. It can be impacted by students' past experiences in a mathematics class—both good and bad. Therefore, the climate you create and the tone you set early is of critical importance. You will want to create an environment that is welcoming and open to mistakes as well as one in which all students' strengths and weaknesses are accepted and supported.

The third basic need—fun—is easy enough to meet. There are numerous opportunities for fun when learning mathematics. They can be as simple as telling a funny story as a lead-in to your lesson, using a favorite manipulative to learn a new mathematics concept, or incorporating a mathematics game as a review. They can be as unique to your school as the events that students attend during the year. The path of a football at the homecoming game lends itself well to the investigation of quadratic functions. The sale prices that students are paying for their dresses for the school dance make for interesting problems involving percentages. Learning may be serious business, but don't miss the chance to sprinkle it with a bit of fun as frequently as possible.

> Students who feel as if they "belong" in your classroom are more likely to put effort into their learning.

The fourth need, freedom, takes some explaining in this context. Freedom in a classroom may be exhibited by students choosing the educational activities they will work on after finishing an assignment, such as exploring educational software related to mathematics or doing a mathematics puzzle. They can be given the freedom to choose their own seats or to choose their own partners for a particular project. Even a regular, optional challenge assignment gives students freedom to do only the optional assignments that are really interesting to them.

The last basic need, power, can better be described as competence or success in the classroom. Students who feel that they are good at mathematics will feel empowered in your classroom, be less likely to fear asking "stupid" questions, and be more willing to present solutions on the board. This feeling of competence comes from students' perceived view of how others see them—both the teacher and their classmates. Students gain power or rank in the classroom in various ways. They can gain power in obvious ways such as by getting the highest grade on a quiz or exam. They can also gain power in simple ways such as by answering a question in class correctly or by contributing to the solution in a cooperative learning setting. When students are observed performing competently, their perceived rank in the class increases.

A word of caution: It is true that increasing students' feelings of power in your classroom should be one of your highest-level goals, and that students who are empowered in mathematics can accomplish truly amazing things, far beyond what you can probably imagine at this point. Yet in your quest to instill power in your classroom, don't make the mistake of widening the gap between the haves and the have-nots. Your brightest students, the ones who always get the As on the quizzes and tests, are not the ones you necessarily need to empower. They are likely already empowered. It is the other students, the ones who lack confidence in their abilities, that you need to turn your attention toward.

There are ways to empower these learners as well; it may just take a bit of creativity. Teachers can effectively increase a student's feelings of competence by providing encouragement. Pointing out a nice solution method to a student, whether in private or to the entire class, can go a long way toward increasing confidence in a student who is uncertain of his or her mathematical ability. Teachers can also influence the mathematical status of a student in the class. Let's consider the case of Miss Gold and her student Rich, who is struggling in her mathematics class.

VIGNETTE 3: INCREASING A STUDENT'S CONFIDENCE IN MATHEMATICS

Seeing that Rich was having some trouble understanding, Miss Gold asks him to come in at lunch for extra help. When he comes, she helps him solve a problem, and she lets him know that she will ask him to write his solution on the board the next day. The next day, she assigns several problems to be written and explained on the board, making sure she includes the problem she discussed with Rich the day before. Rich solves his assigned problem beautifully and seems very happy and confident of his work. Over the next few weeks, he continues to ask Miss Gold for help at lunch or after school and volunteers to put more problems on the board.

The strategy used by Miss Gold allowed Rich to demonstrate his correct solution to the class without having to reveal to his peers that he had received help on this problem the day before. As a result of this one step toward improving confidence, Miss Gold helped Rich to feel better about his mathematical abilities. Rich then began to take responsibility for his own learning by continuing to ask for help. By volunteering to put more problems on the board, he increased his status in the class, thus developing stronger feelings of competence. By one simple action, Miss Gold had encouraged Rich to take more initiative in his learning and to believe in himself and in his success in mathematics. That is the kind of power a teacher should ultimately be seeking to promote.

A FRESH LOOK AT MATH CLUBS AND MATH JEOPARDY

Now that we have described Glasser's (1998) Five Basic Needs, let's revisit the two popular mathematics activities: Math Clubs and Math Jeopardy. Recall that Mr. Herrera was unsatisfied with the outcome of the math contest that his students had participated in. He had thought that offering a math club would be fun and that students would become better problem solvers by participating in contests.

That summer, Mr. Herrera spent a bit of time thinking about the Math Club, and he contemplated whether his goals for the club were in line with the interests and talents of the students in his school. Mr. Herrera had just finished reading about Glasser's Five Basic Needs in *Choice Theory* (1998) (a book suggested by his principal), and he began to reflect on these needs in light of the outcomes of the Math Club the year before. What he began to realize was that most of his students' needs for fun were not being addressed. In addition, consistently scoring eight out of thirty on exams was not exactly conducive to developing students' confidence in their mathematical knowledge; hence it didn't help to meet their need for power.

He eventually came to the conclusion that his primary goal should not be to groom the top math students in the entire school to win local, state, and national math contests, but to develop students' interest and love for mathematics. Very few students are destined to be contest winners, but very many students can benefit from becoming interested in math as a result of the Math Club and can go on to take more math classes in high school and college.

The following year he revised his approach to the Math Club, and, instead of using the Math Club for solving problems on practice contests, he used the time for students to explore very rich, open-ended mathematical situations. He carefully chose problems that lent themselves to a variety of approaches and enabled success at different levels as well. With these problems, freshmen in Algebra I could engage in the problem at one level, and seniors in advanced mathematics or calculus could engage in the same problem at a completely different level, with all levels leading to progress and success.

Week after week, students grappled with the problems, often spending more than one session on a rich scenario. They continually amazed Mr. Herrera with the approaches that they used and the insights that they gained from their solution methods. A common way to wrap up the problem was to have a "gallery walk," where students would make posters of their methods and solutions and post them around the room so that all students could view each other's work.

Mr. Herrera reflected at the end of the year on how proud students were of their solutions, especially when they had come up with an approach that no one else had used. But the best parts about the Math Club? There were two: hearing from other teachers as well as the principal that students were often talking excitedly about the Math Club, and speaking to numerous parents who had sought him out to thank him for offering an extracurricular activity that promotes interest in mathematics.

Now let's look at the changes Mr. Hammond decided to make with his Math Jeopardy game. After reflecting on the outcomes, he came to the conclusion that this game had not encouraged the majority of the class to work hard to solve the problems. Because Jeopardy is a game of speed, the students who solved problems more slowly were not confident enough in their abilities to work each problem through to completion, believing that the quicker students would beat them to the answer anyway. More often than not, one of the quicker students on each team was responsible for solving most of the problems correctly, while the others did little but become frustrated. Mr. Hammond took some time to consider the intended outcomes of this game. He hoped that it would help students review the mathematics concepts in the unit and increase their confidence in the knowledge they had gained. As a secondary goal, he hoped his students would have fun solving the mathematics problems in a competitive atmosphere.

Finally, he made two seemingly minor rule changes. First, in order for a team to win points, two people on the team had to solve the problem. The second rule change was that once the winning team was awarded the points, all the other teams in the class could finish the problem for half the total points.

What was accomplished by these simple rule changes? They instituted very important principles for including everyone in the activity. First, because two team members had to solve the problem, it sent out a clear message that everyone could not simply rely on the smartest team member, that the solution had to be truly a group effort. Second, it lessened the effect of the element of speed in the game, thus encouraging the rest of the class not to give up. Even though a group might not have been the quickest in solving the problem, if they were diligent and finished the problem, they had the chance to collect half the points. Thus, for each question, every team could feel successful by winning at least half the allotted points. By incorporating these simple rule changes, Mr. Hammond took a classic game dependent on speed and turned it into a game with more winners, thus promoting more positive feelings toward the mathematics game and, ultimately, more confidence in the students' mathematical abilities.

It is also important to remember what was discussed earlier: The high-achieving student does not need help in becoming empowered as much as the average- or low-achieving student. It is often the case that we give out accolades to the first person to get the answer. What message does that send to many other students who may have been able to solve the problem, given a little more time? It may teach them not to try harder, because they believe they have very little chance of defeating the quickest students, who seem to always be the first ones to get it right.

These two examples demonstrate how knowledge of Glasser's Five Basic Needs can be used to guide decisions on engaging all learners. Creating a classroom climate conducive to including every student can be accomplished by first considering what your goals are for each classroom activity. If your activity is not producing the intended outcomes, then you need to ask yourself this question: Which of the five basic needs is this activity not meeting for my students? As demonstrated earlier, the activity may need only some minor adjustments to increase student participation.

Glasser's Five Basic Needs provide a foundation for our philosophy of engagement. If you consider the needs of the

Glasser's Five Basic Needs

1. Survival
2. Love and belonging
3. Fun
4. Freedom
5. Power

students in your class, and you design your lesson with their needs in mind, your intended outcome—that of including everyone in learning mathematics—will be closer to being realized. With Glasser's Five Basic Needs in mind, let's further inspect affective issues specific to the domain of mathematics.

AFFECTIVE ISSUES RELATED TO TEACHING AND LEARNING MATHEMATICS

You have seen that the Five Basic Needs are general in that they can relate to any classroom. Yet these needs have particular relevance in a mathematics classroom, where emotions play a big role in students' attitudes toward learning mathematics. Research has found that students' past experiences in learning mathematics influence their disposition toward further learning in this area (Sliva & Roddick, 2001). Before students arrive in a classroom, their mathematical experiences have helped to form their beliefs about their mathematical abilities. Students experience both positive and negative emotions while learning mathematics, and these emotions influence the development of their attitudes toward mathematics as a whole. Many students who are struggling with mathematics experience mathematics anxiety, and it can be very challenging for both the student and the teacher to undo these feelings of anxiety toward the subject. Because affective variables can impact a student's learning of mathematics, strategies for fostering a positive attitude toward mathematics should be used in instruction.

Attitudes Toward Learning Mathematics

Four affective issues often arise when learning mathematics: (1) the role of the teacher; (2) support and influence of family; (3) challenge; and (4) issues of fear, failure, and avoidance (Sliva & Roddick, 2001). All four of these issues have great potential to influence a student's attitude toward learning mathematics and should be recognized as such. Throughout this book we focus on the role of the teacher in learning mathematics. In the section to follow, "Getting to Know Your Students," we briefly discuss the role of the family. We touched on the issues of challenge and fear when we discussed Glasser's Five Basic Needs, and we expand on these ideas here in relation to learning mathematics.

The issues of challenge and fear are ones that hit home for many students in mathematics classes. Challenge can be any situation in which students are asked to compete with themselves or their peers to demonstrate their understanding of mathematics topics. Fear often results from failing at a given challenge, thus creating a desire to avoid such challenge and negative feelings in the future.

Of course, the use of challenge can be both positive and negative. For some students, the experience of having to compete with their peers is devastating and can create detrimental effects on their feelings toward mathematics and their perceived ability to learn the subject. These students may be fearful of any challenge and become afraid of failing in mathematics. For others, challenge is a driving force in shaping their positive attitudes toward mathematics. It is important for the teacher to be sensitive to each student's personality and how he or she responds to challenge, especially in mathematics.

Students whose last memory of learning mathematics resulted in fear or failure will likely have quite different perceptions about learning further mathematics than students who recall a more positive resolution to a difficult situation in a mathematics class. Above all, in addition to greater mathematical understandings, you, as a teacher, want your students to leave with fond memories of your mathematics class.

Because affective variables can impact a student's learning of mathematics, strategies for fostering a positive attitude toward the subject should be used in instruction. The following list is a compilation of instructional techniques for addressing affective issues (Mercer & Mercer, 1998; Montague, 1997):

- ❖ Involve students in setting their own goals, and support students in understanding their responsibility and role in their own learning. If students are engaged in determining their own learning goals, they often begin to take personal responsibility for their learning rather than seeing it as something out of their control. These goals should be challenging yet attainable.
- ❖ Make learning meaningful. Provide problems that are relevant to students' lives, so that they connect with the mathematics you are teaching.
- ❖ Model enthusiasm toward learning mathematics and solving mathematical problems.
- ❖ Have students write about their attitudes and feelings toward mathematics.
- ❖ Provide the opportunity for students to demonstrate what they have learned for other students, and teach them to compliment one another for trying hard and being successful.
- ❖ Deemphasize goals that foster competition among students. Avoid publicizing grades based on comparisons among students.

Because students differ in their motivation, self-perception, and attitudes, strategies for increasing positive attitudes toward learning mathematics will vary, depending on the student. An important component in maintaining a positive attitude toward learning mathematics is to create a classroom environment that is conducive to learning for all students. Students must feel that if they fail, they will not be punished or ridiculed by the teacher or other peers. A discussion in the first few days of school about the types of behavior that are acceptable in the class should also include specifics about how students are to treat each other. Mistakes should be treated as avenues to success.

Getting to Know Your Students

It is important to recognize the influence of the family on students' beliefs about learning mathematics. Contacting parents or guardians of students may be very useful in determining more about their lives outside of school. Often, learning about home expectations can provide a new perspective on how to more effectively teach the student.

As a teacher, it is important to be understanding and flexible about the needs your students may have. These efforts will go a long way toward gaining their respect and the support of parents and guardians. Many students may not come from homes with parents who can help them with mathematics homework or projects; some may come from homes where English is not the first language or is not spoken at all, and many will not come from homes that support the belief that education is important. Getting to know your students as individuals and knowing their strengths and weaknesses in learning mathematics will help you facilitate their learning.

The most important thing to remember is to take an interest in who your students are and value them for who they are. Make sure students know that they are valued, no matter what their cultural background, first language, gender, or strengths and weaknesses in mathematics. When your students come to feel a sense of belonging in their classroom, you will make great strides in creating a positive learning environment and, in addition, you will encourage engagement in learning mathematics.

> The most important thing to remember is to take an interest in who your students are and value them for who they are.

STUDENTS ENGAGED IN LEARNING PROBABILITY

So far we have looked at important affective components in the mathematics classroom and what may be done to create a positive learning environment. Next we will take a look at the behavioral and cognitive domains. We begin this discussion by looking at a mathematics class that is studying probability. This scenario will help us to begin thinking about the different behavioral and cognitive components that help to make a lesson engaging.

In the lesson outlined below, the seniors are given a real-world problem-solving scenario that they can analyze using probability. Students are asked to create different games, make predictions about the expected outcomes, and provide mathematical justifications for the results. Included in this lesson are conceptual as well as procedural notions of probability, in addition to a distinction between experimental results and expected (theoretical) results based on mathematical principles.

Charity Challenge

The seniors at Niskayuna High School are required every year to organize a charity event for their community service graduation requirement. They have decided that all proceeds will go to a local food bank. This year, they have decided to create a community carnival where there will be a blueberry pancake breakfast, face painting, a field event, and carnival games for all ages. They have worked hard to get local businesses to donate food, prizes, and their employees' time to this event. The seniors are required to orchestrate the entire event from start to finish, and it is an event that takes many months to plan. One of the many components of this event is designing games. They have decided there will be a variety of games, two of which they will work on this particular week in mathematics class. Since the class had been studying probability, their teacher, Mr. Edwards, thinks it is appropriate to have them create games with which they could make money and to predict how much money they could make. With these games, they could apply the mathematical concepts of probability and expected value.

Two different games are to be created using simple items: two dice and a Velcro dart board with balls. Students are to create versions of the games so that the "house" (in this case the senior class) wins an overwhelming number of times so that they make money. (Such a game is unfair to the individual playing). They are to first think about what a fair game would look like and then adapt it to be a winning game for the charity event. In each of these cases, they must verify that the game actually works the way it was intended to, and they must justify the reasoning that brought them to this conclusion. At the end of the activity, the class is to vote on which of the invented games to use at the carnival.

Mr. Edwards tells the students that they are required to present and defend their findings to the class and turn in a written copy to him. Since the students have worked on basic probability over the past few weeks, they quickly go to work in their groups on the assignment. As the groups work, some visit the cabinets in the back of the room to get some dice and graphing calculators.

One group offers their answer almost immediately, saying that all you need to do to make a fair game is to have half of the outcomes winners and half of the outcomes losers. An adjustment to make the seniors win more than half the time would be simple. "What are the possible outcomes?" Mr. Edwards challenges them, to which they reply, "whatever you get when you roll the two dice." "But are you adding the numbers on the two dice, subtracting them, or what? You are in charge of making up the rules of your own game." Students think about that for a few moments and then go back to work to figure out some possible solutions.

Previous Lessons

In previous mathematics lessons, the students had played the two-dice game to learn about probability, and they had completed both tables shown in Figure 3.1 (one for an addition game and the other for a multiplication game). Students had learned that a mathematical analysis of the possible sums of numbers indicated by two rolled dice includes exactly 18 even and 18 odd sums. Hence, rolling dice could be made into a fair game by determining even sums to be a winning roll and odd sums to be a losing roll. Students had also learned that the possible products of numbers indicated by two rolled dice included 27 even outcomes and only 9 odd outcomes; hence a dice-rolling game would not be fair if even products were determined to be a winning roll and odd products to be a losing roll. Although they understood the theoretical probability of rolling different sums and products, students had not spent much time on expected values. Mr. Edwards had planned to further their understanding of expected value during the planning of the carnival games.

Initial Conclusions

As Mr. Edwards circulates around the room, he notices that another group has picked up on the first group's comment on adapting a fair game. Their game has the following rules:

It will cost $1 to play the game for one roll of the two dice. If you get an even sum of the two dice you win $1 and if you get an odd sum with the two dice you lose $1.

Mr. Edwards is happy with their attempt, but he wants them to consider what it means to "lose $1." He notices that nobody in the group

Figure 3.1 Possible Outcomes for Throws of Dice

Possible Outcomes for the Sum of Two Dice

	1	2	3	4	5	6
1	2	3	4	5	6	7
2	3	4	5	6	7	8
3	4	5	6	7	8	9
4	5	6	7	8	9	10
5	6	7	8	9	10	11
6	7	8	9	10	11	12

Possible Outcomes for the Product of Two Dice

	1	2	3	4	5	6
1	1	2	3	4	5	6
2	2	4	6	8	10	12
3	3	6	9	12	15	18
4	4	8	12	16	20	24
5	5	10	15	20	25	30
6	6	12	18	24	30	36

considered the fact that you have to pay $1 to play, and that amount needs to be taken into account when calculating expected value. He asks the group to check out the validity of their proposed game by simulating it using a probability simulator on a graphing calculator. He instructs them to play the game 200 times and determine how much money is won or lost.

"Mr. Edwards," one student says after 10 minutes. "I am not getting what I thought I would get when I use my graphing calculator."

"Well!" Mr. Edwards exclaims. "There seems to be a discrepancy between the theoretical and experimental results. What could be happening?" When no one responds, he thinks for a moment, and then he says, "Why don't you carefully go over your approach and make sure that everything is taken into account?"

Students in this group go back to work, and Mr. Edwards notices that other groups are having similar problems making significant progress on this project. After 15 more minutes, he decides that it is a good time to bring the class back together to discuss some of the issues they have been grappling with.

"Let's come back together as a group to discuss the progress you have been making in your groups and to clarify any issues or questions that have arisen," he says. Mr. Edwards asks for volunteers to communicate their findings, and one group explains its findings in this way:

We thought we would follow the first group's suggestion and work on the fair game first, because that seemed to be the easiest for us. We remember that when you look at the sum of two dice, half of the sums are even and the other half are odd, so we thought that would make a fair game. You could win $1 when you roll an even sum and lose $1 when you roll an odd sum. Then we checked our game out by playing it on the calculator 200 times. We organized the results in a payout table for different numbers of players.

The group shares their table of the outcomes of the sum of two dice after rolling the dice 200 times (see Figure 3.2).

Since the number of even and odd outcomes was roughly the same, winning or losing $1 occurred almost equally often, which seems to make it a fair game. But what the table doesn't show is that, when 200 people play the game, they each have to pay $1. That is $200 for the seniors right off the bat! And since everything after that has an equal chance of happening, then the seniors should expect to win $200 for every 200 players and not just break even. So it's not really a fair game, but I guess it would be okay for the carnival, because the seniors have an unfair advantage.

Figure 3.2 Payout Table for Even and Odd Sums

Number of Players	Number of Even Sums	Number of Odd Sums	Amount Players Win (for even sum)	Amount Carnival Wins (for odd sum)	Total Amount for Carnival
50	31	19	31	19	−12
100	41	59	41	59	18
150	78	72	78	72	−6
200	96	104	96	104	8

When the group finishes their presentations, they have many questions. "What does it mean to lose $1? Is that the dollar that they originally paid?" "Why are they winning $1? Shouldn't they be winning a prize, like a stuffed animal?" and "How much do the stuffed animals cost us? Should we have different sizes of stuffed animals like they do at real carnivals?"

Refining the Outcomes

Mr. Edwards realizes at this moment that students understand part of the "moral" to this story, as there is a moral to most of the mathematical activities, or "stories," that he uses in his classroom. The moral that students are realizing in this activity is that textbook problems for the most part are clearly defined and work out cleanly. Real-life problems, on the other hand, are often quite unclearly defined and do not work out quite so cleanly as their textbook counterparts. There are often many decisions that need to be agreed upon before proceeding appropriately. As well, there are often solutions that have to be adapted or abandoned completely based on the decisions that are made.

The class takes several minutes to discuss the issues raised. Eventually the class realizes that part of the confusion lies in the definition of "losing" $1. Does it mean that they lose the dollar that they pay to play, or that they have to give up another dollar? Everyone laughs at this thought and agrees that the player would just lose the dollar that he or she paid to play. Thus, if players win a dollar, then they actually just break even, since they get the dollar back that they paid to play. Most students also agree that it would not be a very fun game if your dollar were simply returned to you and that you should win a stuffed animal instead. Mr. Edwards tells the class that the small stuffed animals the school buys cost 50 cents each and that the large stuffed animals cost $2 each.

Once students finish this discussion, Mr. Edwards sends them back to their groups to work on making adjustments to their games. At this point the period is almost over, and he asks the students to work on their games for homework and be ready to discuss their games with their group members the next day.

This activity goes on for two more days, and students come up with a variety of solutions. Once they decide on the rules for their games, they have to play them, simulate them with graphing calculators, or use theoretical probability to determine the "expected value," which is the amount they expect to win from each game. One game the groups develop is given here:

It will cost $1 to play the game for one roll of the two dice. If the product of the numbers shown on the two dice is even, you lose the $1 you paid to play; if the product is odd, you win a small stuffed animal (costing 50 cents).

Students justify this game in the following manner. If 200 people play the game, then the seniors will initially collect $200. Since $\frac{3}{4}$ of the outcomes are even, $\frac{3}{4} \times 200$, or 150, people would be expected to lose. Since $\frac{1}{4}$ of the outcomes are odd, $\frac{1}{4} \times 200$ or 50 people would be expected to win a small stuffed animal. Fifty stuffed animals will cost $50 \times (.50) = \$25$, so the total amount the seniors would expect to make for 200 students playing the game will be about $175.

Creating Another Game Using Geometric Probability

Mr. Edwards was impressed with the efforts of his students. In the end they agreed that the games were a lot harder to solve than they originally had thought they would be. Since they had already studied probability with rolling two dice, they thought they knew everything there was to know already. Once they conquered the two dice games, however, they were ready to move on to something even more challenging: using geometric probability to create a dart board game.

The following dart board game was presented to them:

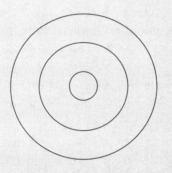

The radius of the small circle is 1 inch.

The radius of the next larger circle is 3 inches.

The radius of the largest circle is 5 inches.

You win $10 for hitting in the center circle.

You win $5 for hitting within the next area.

You win $1 for hitting in the outer area.

Investigate whether or not this is a winning game. Decide how much money people should pay to play the game. Then adapt the game for the carnival.

Students spent a day working on the dart board game and came up with a variety of workable solutions to use at the carnival. (See Appendix C for possible solutions.)

Revisiting the Affective Domain

Before we discuss the behavioral and cognitive domains, let's briefly discuss the affective issues at play in this activity. We have purposefully chosen a lesson in probability related to the community carnival, but we would like to stress that lessons do not have to be unique to be engaging. Teachers who are experienced in promoting a positive attitude in their students and in encouraging their students to be active in their learning can take any lesson and make it engaging. Let's look at the specifics of what Mr. Edwards did to engage students in this lesson.

First, he began by involving all of the learners in a problem-solving scenario that was interesting to them: the upcoming carnival. The students were intrigued and felt a sense of pride in helping to create the games that would be used at the carnival. By using this scenario, Mr. Edwards helped to instill in his students a positive attitude toward learning mathematics. This set the tone for the affective factor related to engagement.

He continued to encourage his students by announcing that the students would be choosing the best games to use at the carnival, thus instilling in them a desire to do well in addition to creating an interest in the games made by other classmates. Furthermore, Mr. Edwards treated all students with respect and entertained all questions in a nonjudgmental manner. It is obvious by observing just one lesson that his students respect him as their teacher and feel comfortable asking and answering questions as well as expressing any confusion they might be experiencing.

ENGAGING LEARNERS IN THE BEHAVIORAL DOMAIN

The primary format for traditional mathematics instruction has been the lecture. Typically, a teacher lectures on the topic of the day, shows the class several examples, and then the class practices the skills demonstrated in the lecture. In reform-based mathematics classrooms today, there is an increasing emphasis on interaction and student communication. These differences are reflected in the way the teacher presents material as well as in the roles the students play in the class. In a lecture-style class, the student is responsible for little more than listening (and possibly taking notes) and practicing problems similar to the ones done on the board during the lecture. The teacher is assumed to be the person who holds all the knowledge, and his or her job is to dispense it to the students.

In the Charity Challenge scenario, Mr. Edwards's role in the classroom was a bit different than that of lecturer. He did not just present the lesson while his students watched; instead, he involved his students in the learning activity. He was more of a facilitator of learning than the sole holder of knowledge. In his role of facilitator, he promoted communication through his questioning techniques as well as through his use of cooperative learning in the lesson. Note that Mr. Edwards was careful not to answer all questions posed to him without challenging his students to think on their own. For example, when students were confused about how to deal with all the questions they had about creating the games, he did not simply tell them the answers and proceed with the next item on the lesson plan. He allowed time for students to discuss their confusion and seek clarity on the issues before moving on. Mr. Edwards used questioning techniques to engage his students in constructing their own understanding.

Mr. Edwards also had his students work in groups to solve the problem. He created a structure for student mathematical communication and participation both within small groups and with a larger group. The act of grouping his students together during the problem-solving process encouraged students to interact with each other and to discuss the problem verbally. Cooperative learning (appropriately structured and implemented) is a good way to encourage mathematical discussions among classmates.

At the onset, it may be difficult to have your students work effectively in cooperative groups. However, with the help of a few techniques, this process can be improved. First, you must ensure that the activity you have selected is conducive to cooperative learning: Such activities are those that can be approached in a variety of ways or that involve more than one person in collecting, recording, and analyzing data. Keeping in mind what you know about your students, group them carefully, assign roles and responsibilities, use a self-evaluation tool for each student after each cooperative learning activity, and discuss appropriate participation. Mr. Edwards's class was a senior class adept at working cooperatively, so much of the cooperative learning appeared seamless.

One of the important features of cooperative learning is that every student needs to participate to make it successful. All students may not bring the same skills to the table, yet all students should participate at some level. A student who is unsure how theoretical probability relates to expected outcomes is still able to participate in collecting and recording the data by actually playing the game or simulating it on a calculator. He or she may need some assistance from the other group members to analyze the results, yet the student will have been able to fully participate up to that point and can take more of a learning role in the analysis phase.

When you are creating lessons for your students, behavioral components of engagement are important to consider. Cooperative learning is an extremely effective behavioral approach to engaging students, one that will reap rewards on the cognitive and affective levels as well. The more that your students actively participate in what they are learning, the more likely they are to remember the lesson, and the more likely it is that they will enjoy themselves and become engaged in learning mathematics.

ENGAGING LEARNERS IN THE COGNITIVE DOMAIN

As you may remember from our earlier discussion, the cognitive components in engagement relate to the mental effort and processing expended while learning something new. The quality of that mental effort involved in learning mathematics can be enriched in many ways. We begin by describing the use of multiple representations to engage learners using manipulatives. Manipulatives offer a means to represent mathematics concretely. Subject-specific technology, such as graphing calculators and mathematics software, also serves to promote cognitive engagement in learning mathematics. We also focus on using problem solving to increase the mental effort students expend in their learning tasks.

Multiple Representations

Using multiple representations involves the presentation of a concept in different ways to promote understanding among more students. For example, when teaching a new concept, a teacher may use words, diagrams, pictures, equations, graphs, or symbolic representations. Students often need multiple methods of viewing a concept to understand it. Our discussion of Bruner's philosophy of learning in Chapter 2 focused on the idea that learners develop understanding of a concept by moving through three distinct modes of learning: the concrete (hands-on), pictorial, and symbolic modes. As students develop their understanding of mathematics, their repertoire of representations increases and becomes more varied. For example, in the carnival activity, students could use concrete representations, like dice (and dart boards), to help them determine the outcomes of the game; they could also use tables and graphs or a graphing calculator. If students are having difficulty with a concept, revisiting the concrete level may help facilitate their understanding.

Manipulatives: These mathematical tools are a means to provide concrete explorations (the hands-on mode) for students in order to make mathematics more accessible. Mr. Edwards provided students with a hands-on experience with probability experiments by allowing them to conduct an experiment with actual dice. Most seniors were ready to investigate probability at an abstract level, yet they were able to strengthen their understandings and corroborate their results by performing actual experiments. The use of the dice helped to form a stronger connection between experimental and theoretical probability.

Technology: Although some school districts may not emphasize or require the use of technology in learning mathematics, it can be an integral part of a student's mathematical learning. Experience has shown that technology can be used to facilitate learning mathematics in a variety of ways. Simple calculators can be used for developing number sense as well as for solving problems involving large numbers. Graphing calculators may be used in middle and high school to describe and analyze real-life data using graphs of functions as well as statistical graphs. Graphing calculators and other computer software may be used to simulate probability experiments and otherwise demonstrate concepts visually. In addition, virtual manipulatives are available online for further enrichment of concepts learned with actual manipulatives in class.

The graphing calculator was used in the Charity Challenge scenario as a tool to explore more repetitions of the experiment than could be done by hand. This allows students whose data may not be representative of the theoretical probabilities to observe that larger data sets often more closely approximate theoretical outcomes. It also helps students develop an understanding of the concept of expected value. Students were able to use the calculator to investigate the amount of money made at their games for different numbers of players.

**Benefits of
Technology for Students**

❖ Visually demonstrates concepts

❖ Brings real-life data into the classroom

❖ Engages learners

Although there are many benefits to using technology, it is important to remember that technology should be used as an instructional tool to increase students' understanding of mathematics and not just for the sake of using technology. Using technology allows you to easily demonstrate concepts in a visual manner and to engage learners, which can help reach a wider range of students.

Problem Solving

Another strategy to support student engagement in the cognitive domain is problem solving. Students who are learning interesting mathematics and are continually challenged to the peak of their ability levels are more likely to thrive in the classroom.

Mathematically speaking, students need to be exposed to both conceptual and procedural understandings, and they can benefit at all levels from seeing mathematics as a connected body of knowledge. Incorporating the use of problem solving in your lessons will allow you to challenge more students on different cognitive levels. It is good to remember that problem solving can range from simple word problems to complex, open-ended tasks. Problem solving should be an experience unlike solving exercises: Typically, students have not solved the types of problems given to them in problem-solving scenarios. In addition, if the problem solving is within a meaningful context, it will be more engaging to the learner.

Bloom's taxonomy is one well-known classification scheme that describes a hierarchy of six levels of cognitive objectives: knowledge, comprehension, application, analysis, synthesis, and evaluation. The taxonomy has been updated to address current educational research, and the new levels are as follows: remembering, understanding, applying, analyzing, evaluating, and creating (Anderson & Krathwohl, 2001).

In most textbooks, there are plenty of knowledge (remembering), comprehension (understanding), and, to a lesser extent, application (applying) problems. It is much harder to find rich problems that challenge students to perform at the three higher levels. Providing rich problems gives students opportunities to analyze the problem situation, evaluate their methods and the reasonableness of the solution, and synthesize, which involves the creation of a new understanding or outcome.

Creating the games in the Charity Challenge involved all levels of Bloom's taxonomy. In the Shake Across America vignette, students were also called upon to incorporate the higher levels of Bloom's taxonomy. In an extension students were asked to solve the problem in two different ways, to compare the two different approaches and evaluate the reasonableness of their two answers.

The key to cognitive engagement is to use methods that promote deeper thinking about the mathematical topics students are learning. Rather than leading students toward solving their problems in one particular way or presenting problems in only one format, it is more effective to teach students general problem-solving skills and to use multiple representations of mathematical concepts and content. These teaching methods create a cognitively richer experience that can engage your students and ultimately help them succeed in mathematics. Thinking back to the Charity Challenge scenario, the students were engaged in a real-life problem that had a variety of answers. It is a true problem-solving scenario, as there were many different questions that needed to be answered, and students had to analyze and synthesize at many different places in the problem.

SUMMARY

In this chapter, we focused on the three components of engagement: the affective, behavioral, and cognitive components. Although we looked at each factor separately, it is important to realize that all of these components are intertwined. Students who are engaged cognitively at the appropriate level have more opportunities for success in mathematics than those who are not so engaged, and this engagement improves their attitude toward the subject. In turn, active engagement in communication about mathematics tends to influence understanding as well. Paying attention to each factor will serve you well in creating a positive classroom environment.

4 Engagement Strategies for Special Populations

In this chapter we will discuss the following:

- ❖ The Special Needs Learner
- ❖ The Gifted Learner
- ❖ The English Language Learner

VIGNETTE 1: DISPARATE LEARNERS IN ALGEBRA I

Mrs. Penny is quite frustrated as her Algebra I class comes to an end. This particular lesson did not go well. Today she was teaching how to graph linear equations. Her students were required to take equations in standard form, place them in slope intercept form, and graph them on a coordinate plane. She knew this was going to be difficult when she began the class, as many students in the class were still struggling with fractions, solving equations with one variable, coordinate graphing, and standard form. It was also going to be challenging because she knows there are several students who will understand what she is saying immediately and others who will not even begin to grasp what she is teaching. However, she does not feel she has the time to go back and reteach the prerequisite skills necessary for all of her students to be ready for this lesson. She also feels that to do so would hold back her other students who are ready to learn this material.

Additionally, she knows several of her students could use more than one day to learn the material due to learning challenges as well as language barriers. In this class she has 32 students—about half the students understood the concept and will be successful with their homework; about 8 of them could use more help, but could get it with a little more help and time; and the rest she fears may never understand what she taught, as they are so far behind and she does not know where she will get the time needed to remediate. In this last group of students, four are special needs students, each of whom has an Individualized Education Program (IEP), and two others are English language learners.

On the other end of the spectrum, of the half that understood the material she presented today, at least three understood it immediately and likely could have moved on to a new concept during this class period; they don't need a great deal of practice.

This is a familiar feeling for Mrs. Penny, a feeling of frustration and helplessness with the vast variability in her students' backgrounds and abilities.

Many, if not most of you, have experienced a class like this, and we hope you can get a sense of the challenge for Mrs. Penny. The question that naturally arises from this classroom is: How do you begin to address the needs of such a diverse group of learners? How does one teach and have equity for all? The Equity Principle, which at its core states "Excellence in mathematics education requires equity—high expectations and strong support for all students" (National Council of Teachers of Mathematics, 2000, p. 12), is paving the way for high-quality mathematics instruction for all students. Unfortunately, students with special needs (cognitive, affective, or language based) are often left behind due to the challenges encountered while learning mathematics. Students in most classes range from gifted to below grade level. Some classes have even more extreme ranges, with students on one end being significantly below grade level (many grade levels below) and those at the other end being highly abstract thinkers that could be a grade or two above. In addition to the range in cognitive ability, students may also vary in their English language proficiency. It is a challenge to meet the needs of all of your students, from those on the lower end of the extreme to those who need to be challenged.

Another aspect of diversity that needs to be addressed in classrooms is the diverse cultural needs of students. The United States has rapidly become culturally diverse, and this is reflected in our classrooms. It is important for all teachers to recognize the role a student's culture can play for a student when learning mathematics. Culturally responsive teaching (CRT) is at the core of multicultural education. It is based on the perspective that many schools stifle cultural experiences and perspectives.

Culturally responsive educators believe that differences in culture are a strength rather than a weakness in the classroom. Culturally responsive teaching attempts to establish a culturally relevant community that addresses students' needs (Gay, 2000). If a student's culture is not respected and this respect is not incorporated in the classroom and school, students can feel isolated and are less likely to engage in school and feel part of the community. When teachers take the time to get to know a student as an individual, they will likely learn about the student's cultural background. In Chapter 3 we included suggestions for this in the section "Getting to Know Your Student."

In Chapter 3 we also discussed three components of engagement: the affective, behavioral, and cognitive components. This chapter will address these components for the largest groups of students you may have in your classes: special needs students, English language learners, and gifted/talented students. For each of these groups, we discuss the following strategies, which

> A student's culture can play a significant role in how they learn mathematics.

may be used to effectively teach your students: knowing your learner, creating a positive classroom culture, increasing opportunities for positive communication, and differentiating instructional strategies. As you read, you will probably be able to identify the affective, behavioral, and cognitive components, although they are not delineated.

THE SPECIAL NEEDS LEARNER

Know Your Learner

In this book, the term *special needs learner* refers to students who have been identified as having learning disabilities. These students fall across a spectrum; each is unique and has his or her own defining affective, cognitive, and behavioral characteristics. Although we would like to spend more time on specific special needs, due to the scope of this book, we focus only on general strategies.

When planning instruction to include students with special learning needs, such as those in Mrs. Penny's class, it helps to have an understanding of the attributes that challenge or interfere with learning for each student. As well as speaking with the students' previous mathematics teachers, you may want to speak with other professionals who have had contact with your special needs students in the past, such as psychologists or special education teachers. In addition, documents from these professionals, such as IEPs, will also provide useful information.

Inquiries such as the following are helpful in eliciting useful information from previous teachers:

- ❖ Describe your experience working with this student in mathematics last year.
- ❖ What were this student's strengths and weaknesses in terms of content, problem solving, and attitude toward learning mathematics?
- ❖ How does this student react when it is time for mathematics class? For example, is he excited, or does his demeanor falter?
- ❖ Does she enjoy working in groups?
- ❖ How does she interact with other students?

Create a Positive Classroom Culture

Creating a positive classroom culture supports engagement and the learning of mathematics for all students. The most important aspect here is the belief that the student can and will be successful in mathematics. Without this belief, the student is much less likely to succeed. Research has found that the teacher is the single most important variable in the success of a student (Sliva & Roddick, 2001). It is very important that the teacher not create low expectations for achievement for any student, especially those who have a history of mathematical difficulties, such as students who struggle, students labeled as having special needs on the basis of an IEP, or students with whom the teacher has prior experiences that lead the teacher to believe the student will perform poorly. Often these students have been taught using an inferior curriculum that has not given them the same opportunities as their peers who do not have learning disabilities. Lower expectations rob these students of opportunities to learn. A strong belief that the student can and will learn mathematics can be the single most important aspect of teaching these students.

We have previously addressed the importance of maintaining high standards for all learners. This is critical for special needs learners. It is crucial that teachers establish and maintain high expectations for these learners, as traditionally these students' instruction has lacked content and depth in relation to the instruction of their peers without learning disabilities. Typically, these students have experienced failure in the classroom. Because of this, they are often placed in skills-based classrooms, and, as a result, many of these students never experience a conceptually higher level of mathematics and are left out of reform-based mathematics (Baxter, Woodward, & Olson, 2001; Matthews, 2005). Thus they are not provided with the same opportunities nor expected to participate in activities with their peers, often leading to a lack of engagement. One important guiding principle when engaging these learners is to expect all students to learn both concepts and skills and not to limit any student to just skill-based learning. Expect high-level products and high-level thinking (e.g., writing, proofs, projects, solutions to challenging problems). Without high expectations and high standards for all students, there may be equity issues felt by all learners, which may not contribute to a positive classroom culture. Mrs. Penny should be careful to use the same curriculum—adapted to address the varying abilities of her students—in order to maintain equity and foster a positive classroom environment.

An additional characteristic of special needs students that can impact their ability to learn mathematics is difficulty maintaining a positive attitude (Sliva, 2003). Many special needs students have had failure throughout their experiences learning mathematics and often think they "cannot do mathematics."

As a reminder, the following strategies mentioned in Chapter 3 are helpful with special needs students as well:

❖ Make learning meaningful.
❖ Model enthusiasm toward learning and doing mathematics.
❖ Require students to write about their attitudes and feelings toward learning mathematics.
❖ Provide an opportunity for students to demonstrate for other students what they have learned, and teach them to compliment one another for trying hard and being successful.
❖ Deemphasize goals that foster competition among students.

In most classes, students rapidly learn who are the stronger and the weaker students in the class. For this reason, it is very important to maintain a positive environment. Mrs. Penny may use all of the above strategies to maintain a positive environment for her students. For example, when she is planning, she may think about the relevance of the mathematics she is teaching to her students' lives. In order to make mathematics meaningful, she could use a variety of hands-on strategies to develop understanding as well as add in some real-world applications of the mathematics. For example, Mrs. Penny could use a geoboard as a coordinate plane and have students use rubber bands to create various lines. They could investigate points on the lines and how to get from one point to the next, thereby helping students to understand the rate of change, or slope, of a line. When teaching about linear equations, Mrs. Penny could also include a real-world problem about getting the best buy on a cell phone according to the anticipated usage of talking and texting. She could encourage her students to explore different cell phone plans and to use linear functions to determine which of the plans would be the cheapest.

Increase Opportunities for Communication and Participation

When you read the Charity Challenge scenario in Chapter 3, it's likely that you noticed there were a variety of instructional materials and methods used to include all learners. Special needs students' specific needs were addressed by using strategic groupings and multiple avenues to see the mathematics in different ways. Mr. Edwards used various teaching techniques, such as active participation in group problem solving, simulation of the games on a graphing calculator, visual representation of the outcomes of two dice in a table, and verbal discussion of the results and reasoning related to the experiment.

This example illuminates our suggestions for increasing communication and participation:

❖ Use cooperative groupings (with appropriate placement and structures).
❖ Allow alternative methods to express mathematical ideas.

Research has found that many special needs students have difficulties in the area of language, both with processing and understanding and with expression. Both of these areas may impact a student's participation in class. As demonstrated in the vignette, small-group work, including cooperative learning, has been shown to be effective when engaging these learners. These students will often need encouragement to participate in their learning. Be sure to carefully group students with others who are sensitive to the students' special needs in the areas of communication. In addition, a structure for how students will participate that includes expectations for respect, responsibilities, and communication strategies within groups must also be established. Students with special needs may participate in varying ways; this is to be expected. However, it must be assumed that they will all participate!

In planning for a class like Mrs. Penny's, teachers need to be careful about selecting groups of students to work together. Careful monitoring and feedback should also be utilized to ensure all students are benefiting from the interactions.

Mrs. Penny could encourage her students to use alternative methods to express their thinking, so that she may be able to obtain more information about their mathematical understandings. Students may use manipulatives, such as the geoboards mentioned above, or pictorial representations to express their thinking in large or small groups or even as a one-on-one assessment. In addition, some students may express themselves better verbally than when using a paper and pencil. This is especially true for students who may have visual-processing or motor-processing difficulties. For teachers, it is important to be aware that these students may take longer to respond and need more wait time in the classroom than the other students need.

As it is with all students, learning about the areas of strength and weakness for special needs students is very important, because a teacher will want to teach to students' strengths to address their weakness. For example, if a student has relative strengths in taking in information visually and relative weaknesses receiving information verbally, the teacher will want to represent mathematics visually as well as verbally as much as possible.

> As it is with all students, learning about the areas of strength and weakness for special needs students is very important, because a teacher will want to teach to students' strengths to address their weaknesses.

This will enable the student to increase his or her mathematical knowledge by taking in the information using his or her strength; it will also help the student to strengthen the verbal avenue of receiving information.

Differentiate Instructional Strategies

As we have mentioned, traditional instruction was led by the teacher and "given" to a group of students. Often this instruction was not flexible for the wide range of learners in the classroom. Differentiation of teaching strategies allows the same high-quality instruction to reach all learners, and this instruction is tailored to reach a large spectrum. Teachers may differentiate teaching strategies on the basis of the information gathered and synthesized in the process of knowing their students. This may sound like creating 30 different lesson plans for 30 different students; it need not be. A few easy strategies can help meet the needs of many students.

To begin the process, we suggest gathering the following additional information for these students:

❖ How do the students learn mathematics best? Do they prefer to use hands-on manipulatives, to describe their ideas in spoken words or in writing, or to draw their ideas?

❖ How much prerequisite mathematics content have the students mastered? For example, if the student is going into algebra, prerequisite knowledge may include mastery of the concepts involved in prealgebra, such as conceptual understanding of what variables stand for.

Here are a few suggestions for how to differentiate instructional strategies in the mathematics classroom:

- ❖ Present new concepts using Bruner's model (as discussed in Chapter 2). This research-based sequence of instruction engages learners in a new concept at a concrete level and then progresses to a more abstract level. Special needs students may need varying amounts of time at each of the first couple of levels.
- ❖ Use a think-aloud strategy that enables the teacher to model appropriate behaviors. A teacher that models personal thinking processes and strategies for solving a problem out loud is using the think-aloud strategy.
- ❖ Create a template to isolate information. To remove distractions, create window templates to isolate certain problems, paragraphs, or sentences on a page. The templates may be created on a computer, and students can keep templates in their notebooks for use when needed.

Cognitive research on teaching and learning emphasizes the importance of making connections. Hiebert and Carpenter (1992) state that the degree of a student's understanding is determined by the number, accuracy, and strength of connections. For example, it is useful for students to understand the inverse relationship between multiplication and division, as the concept is used when developing rules for integer operations and for solving equations. Many students with special needs have difficulty making connections when learning mathematics content.

Here are a few strategies for helping these students gain this skill:

- ❖ Use concept maps. A concept map ties newly learned concepts to other mathematical ideas. As students create concept maps, they visually illustrate mathematical connections and describe them in writing.
- ❖ Use graphic organizers. A graphic organizer helps students see patterns within mathematical ideas and generalize them. Graphic organizers also reduce the demand on language.
- ❖ Make connections to other curricular areas. When students interact with mathematics in other disciplines, it can help to strengthen and generalize their understanding of the mathematics. (Chapter 6 contains examples of making connections to other content areas.)

When teaching a class such as Mrs. Penny's, it is important to keep in mind that all students learn at different paces and in different ways, and special needs students are especially vulnerable to pacing issues. Be flexible in your expectations about pacing for different students. Whereas some students may be mastering basic skills, others may be working on more advanced problems. For example, in middle and high school mathematics courses, learners are expected to know how to compute using fractions. But if some students have not mastered this, do not hold them back from other, more complex tasks, such as graphing linear equations. Rather, continue to work in parallel on fractions.

There are many students with special learning needs who may not be identified as such in a school district and therefore may not be eligible for special services. As you learn about all of your students, you may find strategies for your identified students that may also be useful for the rest of your students.

To learn more details and specific information about teaching mathematics to students with special needs, see *Teaching Inclusive Mathematics to Special Learners, K–6*, by Julie A. Sliva (2003).

THE GIFTED LEARNER

In this section we will address the student or students in your class who are well above the average. These are the students in Mrs. Penny's class who understood the information the first time she presented it—the ones who would need little if any assistance in completing the homework and could possibly even move on to another concept or topic in that same class session. The strategies we discuss in this component are similar to the special learner section; however, the questions you may ask and the way you use each of these strategies will be different.

Know Your Learner

Gifted students come from all ethnic and socioeconomic groups, are both male and female, and may not demonstrate their gifts in all content areas. Gifted students demonstrate their talent in mathematics in a range of ways and at varying points in their development. They may differ from their peers by the pace at which they learn. Many gifted learners respond favorably to challenge and have the need for continual intellectual stimulation. You should be careful not to stifle their curiosity or make them feel as if they are a burden because they have different needs. They differ in the depth of their understanding of mathematics; deeper levels of understanding and abstraction are possible for most mathematical topics, so differentiation becomes important. Knowing your gifted students' areas of strength and weakness can help you better tailor their mathematics instruction. In addition to contacting your students' previous teachers and obtaining prior relevant documents, it is wise to seek out any other professionals, such as specialists for gifted learners and counselors in the school, who may have dealt specifically with these students around these issues.

Just as special needs students are not necessarily specifically identified, these students may not be identified as gifted. It is crucial to spot such giftedness early, because if it isn't encouraged, it may never develop.

Students who are gifted in mathematics are likely to demonstrate the ability to

❖ learn and understand mathematical ideas quickly;
❖ be analytical, think logically, and easily see mathematical relationships;
❖ learn and process complex information very rapidly;
❖ identify patterns and make connections between concepts easily;
❖ routinely apply their knowledge in new or unfamiliar contexts;
❖ communicate their reasoning and justify their methods;
❖ ask questions that show clear understanding of, and curiosity about, mathematics;
❖ take a creative approach to solving mathematical problems;
❖ sustain their concentration throughout longer tasks and persist in seeking solutions; and
❖ be more adept at posing their own questions and pursuing lines of inquiry. (Maker, 1982)

Mrs. Penny may improve her teaching for these students by asking questions of their previous teachers so that she may adapt her instructional strategies accordingly. For example, if she has a student who she knows easily gets a concept the first time it is presented, she may want to have specific challenges available to engage the student appropriately. An example of this might be for this student to move directly to an application problem, such as identifying which of three cell phone plans is the best for a certain set of scenarios. It may be far more interesting for this student to complete a real-world problem-solving scenario than to practice the concept with word problems that may seem rather contrived and less interesting to this type of learner. As well, Mrs. Penny may want to steer these students into afterschool or extracurricular activities that involve mathematical or logical reasoning. She should specifically encourage their interest and talent in mathematics. Other options are discussed in the sections below.

Create a Positive Classroom Culture

There are affective issues specific to gifted learners that need to be addressed. The National Association for Gifted Children (NAGC) includes an affective component in their gifted program standards. They suggest that gifted learners be provided with affective curriculum in addition to other services:

> Gifted learners who are comfortable with their abilities are more likely to use their talents in positive ways. High-ability students need specific curriculum that addresses their socioemotional needs and enhances development of the whole child, rather than just focusing on cognitive development. (NAGC, 2005)

NAGC also suggests that gifted learners realize they are different from their peers but have no outlet to discuss these differences and may interpret this difference negatively unless they have assistance in accepting such strengths. Obtaining support for your students from professionals and counselors knowledgeable in this area is suggested. Overall, it is important that these students realize that you value their abilities and encourage their curiosity. It is important to encourage students in their mathematical strengths and not turn them away from mathematics at a young age.

> Gifted learners who are comfortable with their abilities are more likely to use their talents in positive ways.

In Mrs. Penny's class, it was beneficial for her to obtain critical information about the backgrounds of her students prior to school starting, as this information helped her create a positive learning environment. If she had not had this information, a few weeks of school might have passed before she recognized that these students had particular mathematical strengths and that she needed to utilize certain strategies to engage them to create a learning environment that was conducive to their learning. In this short amount of time, some students in her class might have become turned off to the class due to boredom or just feeling out of place. To create this positive environment for these students, she could have made challenges available to them or provided opportunities for them to extend their mathematics learning outside of the classroom in Math Clubs or formal challenges such as Math Counts.

Increase Opportunities for Communication and Participation

It is interesting that promoting communication with gifted learners can also have challenges. Unlike their special needs and English language learner peers, they may absorb information much more quickly, process it more quickly, and as a result want to "go it alone." This can lead to isolation from their peers and from the benefits of working collaboratively in groups. These benefits may include practicing social, communication, and perhaps leadership skills.

Ideally, in cooperative groupings, all gifted students would learn at or near the pace of the quickest pupil, and this would be combined with plenty of communication among group members to sharpen their social abilities. However, this is not always practical, and in many heterogeneous classrooms it can seem like an unlikely scenario. Providing structured groupings with tasks assigned to each member can support more communication for these learners. In addition, it may be important to speak with parents of these students to explain the benefits of group work for their children. Often parents of gifted children will feel that their children are being held back from learning to their fullest potential because they are with "slower" learners. However, these parents are often unaware of the other benefits of cooperative grouping, such as the development of social, communication, and leadership skills.

Ensure that gifted students are not perceived as the "teacher" in their groups and that they are not always responsible for helping out the "slower" students. This can be a very big challenge for any teacher: the balance of cooperative groups. It is especially difficult with gifted students, because a teacher does not want the gifted student in the group to "take charge" of the group and dominate the entire task, or to complete the task on his or her own without the assistance of the group. They want these students to be integral parts of the group and equal contributors. So, Mrs. Penny should not shy away from this important aspect of mathematics class for her gifted students. She does not want to isolate them from their peers nor make them in charge of any group; she wants them to participate equally. Using the information you may obtain from previous teachers and your own anecdotal information and experience from working with these students will be beneficial when designing cooperative groups that work well and increase communication in the classroom.

Differentiate Instructional Strategies

A dilemma facing many mathematics teachers every day is how to make available mathematical opportunities that encourage advanced pursuits of excellence without denying other students access to high-quality mathematics. We need to provide high-level instruction for all learners, including gifted students. In middle and high school, gifted students are often placed into an honors class or accelerated into a higher-level mathematics course. However, you may encounter some students in your classes who have not been accelerated yet are ready for a more challenging experience in mathematics. Such students can investigate the concepts at their grade level more deeply, in addition to furthering their knowledge.

To meet their needs and engage these students, there are several areas in which a teacher may differentiate instruction:

❖ Adjusting the content taught.
❖ Allowing for student preferences.
❖ Altering the pace of instruction.
❖ Creating a flexible classroom environment.
❖ Using specific instructional strategies.

According to Johnson (1993), components of mathematics curriculum for the gifted are as follows:

❖ Content with greater depth and higher levels of complexity.
❖ A discovery approach that encourages students to explore concepts.
❖ A focus on solving complex, open-ended problems.
❖ Opportunities for interdisciplinary connections.

The following are strategies that may be used to differentiate instruction for gifted learners in the mathematics classroom (Johnson, 2000):

❖ Give preassessments so that students who already know the material do not have to repeat it but may be provided with instruction and activities that are meaningful. These assessments should be given in such a way that students have an opportunity to express their understanding either orally or in writing.
❖ Choose textbooks that provide enrichment opportunities. Unfortunately, because most curricula in this country are determined by the textbooks used, and these textbooks are written expressly for the average population, they are not always appropriate for the gifted. No single text will adequately meet the needs of these learners; therefore, teachers need to supplement with multiple resources.
❖ Use inquiry-based, discovery learning approaches that emphasize open-ended problems with multiple solutions or multiple paths to

solutions. Allow students to design their own ways to find the answers to complex questions. More information on this topic can be found in the assessment chapter (Chapter 5).

❖ Use lots of higher-level questions in justification and discussion of problems. Ask "why" and "what if" questions.

❖ Provide units, activities, or problems that extend beyond the normal curriculum. Offer challenging mathematical recreation, such as puzzles and games.

❖ Differentiate assignments. It is not appropriate to give more problems of the same type to gifted students. You might give students a choice of a regular assignment; a different, more challenging one; or a task that is tailored to specific interests.

❖ Provide opportunities to participate in contests such as Mathematical Olympiads.

❖ Bring a variety of speakers into the classroom to explain how mathematics has opened doors in their professions and careers.

❖ Provide some activities that can be done independently or in groups on the basis of student choice. Be careful to provide appropriate instruction for these students and not just let them work on their own, as they too need instruction. Provide useful concrete experiences. Even though gifted learners may be capable of abstraction and may move from concrete to abstract more rapidly, they still benefit from the use of manipulatives and hands-on activities.

It is important to remember that gifted students process information differently, and it is imperative that you focus on their strengths, not their shortcomings. Offer them opportunities that are consistent with their abilities, and challenge them to think and process their new understandings as deeply and comprehensively as they are able.

THE ENGLISH LANGUAGE LEARNER

Know Your Learner

Similar to other special populations of students, these students have a wide range of diversity in their needs, as they often have a great deal of variability in their backgrounds and thus need different pathways for their success. Research has found that it may take as long as seven years to acquire a level of language proficiency comparable to that of native speakers (Collier, 1989; Hartman & Tarone, 1999). The result is that the majority of language minority students do not have access to rigorous subject matter instruction or the opportunity to develop an academic language—the language functions and structures that are needed to understand, conceptualize, symbolize, discuss, read, and write about topics in academic subjects (LaCelle-Peterson & Rivera, 1994). Therefore, it is essential that you learn as much as possible about the previous experiences and backgrounds of your English language learners (ELLs) to engage them and facilitate their learning of mathematics. In addition to assessing their content area knowledge and experiences in learning mathematics, understanding their cultural norms and background is essential to effectively teach them. As is the case for all students, the parents or guardians are rich sources of information, especially in the area of cultural understandings.

You may also want to collaborate with other professionals who have experience working with English language learners. For you as a new teacher of mathematics, working closely with the professional in your school or district responsible for these students can be invaluable. This professional may be called an English as a second language teacher (or an ESL teacher). These individuals should have different and more in-depth knowledge about the student and about teaching ELLs in general. Other professionals in the building who are also teaching the student will also be useful, as they may have learned or know of strategies that will work to reach these students.

Specific Information You May Want to Learn About Your Students

❖ What language do they prefer to use when discussing mathematics?

❖ How well do they work individually, in small groups, in cooperative environments, or in a large group setting?

Create a Positive Classroom Culture

As with the other two populations we have discussed, creating a positive classroom culture is important to engage ELLs in learning mathematics. These learners are also often excluded from high expectations, as it may be difficult to determine their mathematical backgrounds because of language barriers, and it may be assumed that, like their English language skills, their mathematics skills are limited. In addition, ELLs who have mathematics skills that may exceed those of your average students need an environment in which their abilities are valued and supported for further growth. Challenging, age-appropriate lessons provide opportunities for these students.

Second-language acquisition theories address cognitive, affective, and linguistic issues. Affective filters in individuals (created by a variety of factors, such as motivation, self-confidence, or anxiety) can support or disrupt acquisition of a second language (Brown, 2001).

To positively impact these affective issues and thus engage learners in the mathematics classroom, you can do the following:

❖ Create a classroom environment in which learners feel comfortable using and taking risks with English. Incorporate cooperative learning activities that facilitate the building of a positive classroom community. Be sure to integrate your English-speaking students with your ELLs in group activities.

❖ Promote a low-stress classroom culture. It is critical that a mathematics classroom for ELLs be as stress-free as possible. Students need to feel comfortable making mistakes, both in their usage of English and in mathematics, so that they may develop their mathematical thinking. Avoid constant error correction, and include activities that focus on overall ability to communicate meaning.

Increase Opportunities for Communication and Participation

ELLs are at a disadvantage relative to their English-speaking peers in the mathematics classroom. Not having the command of the English language that native speakers do, they may take longer to understand what is asked of them.

The following are strategies for helping these students communicate their mathematical ideas in English and for better supporting their use of different strategies for solving problems (Bresser, 2003):

❖ Modify the way you talk. Specifically, when you are speaking to a class with ELLs, you should speak slowly and use clear articulation. Be sure to stress important words, exaggerate intonation, and use simple words to describe a concept. Be aware of the terms you are using, including any new vocabulary necessary for understanding the lesson.

❖ Build in instructional strategies that focus more on demonstration than on language to support the understanding of new concepts and terms. For example, when teaching a concept such as surface area, present a visual representation, such as pictures, of the concept.

❖ Engage ELLs by including as many opportunities as possible for students to communicate mathematically, both with the teacher and with each other.

❖ Ask questions and use prompts. For example, ask students, What do you think the answer will be? Why do you think that? Can you explain to me how you found your answer? How did you begin the problem? What did you do first? Then what did you do? Can you tell me what the problem is using your own words?

❖ Practice wait time. After you have asked a question, allow sufficient time before you ask a specific student to answer. This will enable all learners, especially ELLs, time to think about the question you are asking, formulate an answer, and respond.

❖ Appropriately state mathematical ideas and concepts in language. As mentioned previously, it is essential to use correct terminology. For example, when teaching about linear equations, be sure to use other terms that represent the concept, such as *function.* However, here is one line of caution: Too many terms can often confuse a student when learning a new concept.

❖ Connect symbols with words. Whenever possible, point to the symbols, such as =, >, and < when you are discussing them. This provides one more possibility for students to strengthen their knowledge and understanding of the symbols and their meaning.

❖ Use Think-Pair-Share. This strategy works well when students are asked to share with a partner, discuss the idea, and then share with the group. In the first step of sharing with a partner, the students are practicing formulating their mathematical thinking as well as their expression of the idea in English, which enables them to alter what they are thinking or saying prior to expressing it to an entire group.

❖ Use English experts. Using this strategy, students explain their thinking in their own language to a more capable English speaker, and then the "English expert" translates the ideas for the teacher. Again, this enables the ELL to practice communication in the classroom with the support of a student who can assist in the translation. Thus, these students are not left out of a discussion.

❖ Encourage students to retell. This strategy enables students to focus on their communication in English primarily and the mathematics secondarily. Ask students to restate and explain, sometimes elaborating on a strategy another student in their group may have used.

❖ Use the buddy system. Allow ELLs to bring an English-speaking peer to the board to support an explanation of a problem.

Think back to Mrs. Malloy's Shake Across America lesson discussed in Chapter 1. She was very committed to all students having equal access to participation in class; therefore, she allowed students to take a peer to the board to assist in explaining the problem. Please note: Not only ELLs may have difficulties explaining or expressing their thoughts; so may other students. Use of manipulatives on the overhead or in small-group situations may also be of assistance for students with these challenges.

It is important to note that although many of these strategies are particularly appropriate for ELLs, they are also useful to increase mathematical communication with all students in your classroom.

Differentiate Instructional Strategies

When teaching a mathematics lesson to ELLs, it is important to build in instructional strategies that focus on demonstration to support the understanding of new concepts and terms.

The following is a list of cognitive strategies that may be used to engage students:

❖ Pose problems in a familiar context. As we mentioned previously, problem solving challenges your learners on many different levels. With a familiarity of structure, ELLs can more easily focus on how to solve the problem rather than on other obstacles that may interfere with their ability to learn mathematics.

❖ Integrate ELLs' culture into lessons whenever possible. Give students opportunities to share examples from schools in their home countries and different ways of learning mathematics.

❖ Make interdisciplinary connections whenever possible, and tap prior knowledge. Connect students' prior knowledge and experiences to new learning. Find out what students already know about a topic by making a concept map on the board. For example, when beginning to teach linear equations, one might want to see how much prerequisite knowledge the student has with regard to related concepts, such as solving single variable equations.

Once again, engagement is an important issue to keep in the forefront of your mind as you teach. The three areas—affective, behavioral, and cognitive—are interrelated in many ways, and all contribute to the engagement of your students in your classroom. An activity follows that embodies the aspects we have discussed with regard to engagement.

EXAMPLE OF ENGAGING LEARNERS IN A MATHEMATICS CLASSROOM

VIGNETTE 2: PERMUTATIONS, COUNTING, AND ICE CREAM CONES

On a very warm June day, Mrs. Wilson was listening to some of the conversations the students were having about the upcoming field day. The students were especially excited that Garrett Farms, a local ice cream store, was coming with many of their ice cream flavors. A couple of students, David and Daniel, were discussing their favorite ice cream and what they might get that day. David said he would choose peanut butter ice cream with chocolate fudge topping and chocolate sprinkles on it. Daniel told him he did not think anyone else would choose exactly the same ice cream cone, flavor, and topping. Mrs. Wilson listened for a minute, and her mind quickly turned to all of the mathematics that was connected to that statement. She had taught probability earlier that year, and she knew she wouldn't be teaching combinations or permutations for the rest of the year. However, she thought an impromptu lesson on permutations and counting principles would tie in nicely with the students' conversation. As she thought about this, she decided to write one question on the board as students were getting ready to leave:

> *How many different single scoop ice cream cones can be made if you know how many different flavors of ice cream, toppings, and cones there are?*

The next day, as the students came into class, Mrs. Wilson began by reminding them that next week was the annual middle school field day and that one of the local ice cream stores, Garrett Farms, was bringing in the ice cream for the field day. Though the owner of the place had many, many flavors in his store and often made seasonal ones just for special occasions, his truck was able to accommodate bringing only 5 flavors of ice cream, 4 different kinds of toppings (chocolate sprinkles, rainbow sprinkles, M&M's, and chocolate fudge), and 3 different kinds of cones (sugar, plain, and waffle). Even though he could not bring all of his flavors, Mr. Garrett and the principal had said, "There are at least 500 different cones that can be made with all of the Garrett Farms ice cream, toppings, and cone choices."

Mrs. Wilson tells the students that over the next couple of days they will be finding out answers to the following questions:

> 1. *How many different ice cream cones can be made if there are 5 different ice cream flavors, 4 different toppings, and 3 different cones? Assume each ice cream cone will contain only 1 scoop of ice cream and 1 topping.*
>
> 2. *What is the probability that your friend would choose exactly the same ice cream cone as you would?*
>
> 3. *How many different flavors, toppings, and cones would Mr. Garrett have to have to make the statement about the 500 different cones true? Identify at least two different ways of determining these figures.*

The students are also told that they might be asked to present their findings to Mr. Garrett and the principal, so they should make sure to justify their statements about the number of different cones.

After Mrs. Wilson presents the problems, she asks the class to brainstorm how they will solve the first problem. When no one raises a hand, she asks if they have ever solved any similar problem in the past. When no one raises a hand even then, she asks the students to think about some general problem-solving strategies that they have used this year to approach many different types of problems. And then she waits.

One student slowly raises her hand. "I remember one problem that had really big numbers, and we had to come up with smaller numbers to try to find a pattern."

"Okay," says Mrs. Wilson, as she writes the strategy on the board. "We can solve a simpler problem."

Other students begin to raise their hands, and Mrs. Wilson writes their suggestions on the board one by one: Use manipulatives to model the problem, make a list, draw a picture, and act it out. She suggests that they break into their groups to attack the first problem using the strategy or strategies of their choosing.

As she walks around the class, she notices the different ways her students are trying to answer the question. Some groups use pictures or manipulatives to represent the choices in the problem. Most decide to create a simpler problem for themselves, since this is a strategy they have previously used. In fact, one group breaks it down to just 2 flavors of ice cream and 3 types of cones. Then they make the problem harder and try 2 kinds of ice cream, 3 cones, and 2 toppings. This group immediately notices a pattern to help them solve the problem.

After a sufficient amount of time has been allowed for investigating the problem, Mrs. Wilson asks for volunteers to share their solutions. The first group shows their work using capital letters as shorthand notation. They used a simplified version of the problem and picked different letters to represent each of the flavors of ice cream, toppings, and cones. They then generated a list of all the different combinations and used their idea of systematic list making to generalize the situation to the original problem given. Another group used a "tree" method. They seemed to realize that, by solving simpler problems (a problem-solving strategy) and drawing trees, the answer could be found by multiplying the three numbers together: $5 \times 4 \times 3 = 60$. One group's explanation includes smaller trees, building to a larger, more inclusive one with the final answer to show how they arrived at their answer (see Figure 4.1). All students arrive at the correct answer, and most seem to understand the generalization using the counting principle.

Since there is time left, Mrs. Wilson asks the students to work on Question 2. This problem does not require much discussion, as they have previously solved probability problems and are quite adept at them. They know they have to use the total number of possibilities from Question 1 and that each student's "own cone" would be one of those possibilities. Since there are 60 different ice cream cones that could be made, the probability that a friend chooses the same cone is $\frac{1}{60}$.

For homework, they are assigned to complete Question 3. They are also asked to write in their journals their thoughts on the following questions:

> How many different ice cream cones can be made if you are allowed to choose 2 flavors, and order matters? 3 flavors? 2 or 3 toppings?

The next day, students investigate how many different ways there are to stack 2 different flavors of ice cream on a single cone. They used the same number of ice cream flavors from the day before, and they also extend their original problem-solving strategies. Students who used trees figure out that they can make a tree with the first branch representing the first flavor and the second branch representing the second flavor. Using the original problem, there are 5 choices for the first scoop of ice cream. Since the ice cream flavors have to be different, there are only 4 choices for the next scoop of ice cream. In total, there are 5 × 4 = 20 different ways to make a 2-scoop ice cream cone, assuming the order of the stacking matters. Students generalize their reasoning so that, if 3 scoops are chosen, there are 5 × 4 × 3 = 60 different ice cream cones that can be made. Similar arguments are made for the number of toppings.

Figure 4.1   Solving a Smaller Problem Using Trees

In this problem there are 2 choices for ice cream flavor, 3 choices for type of cone, and 2 choices for topping. There are 12 different ice cream cones that can be made.

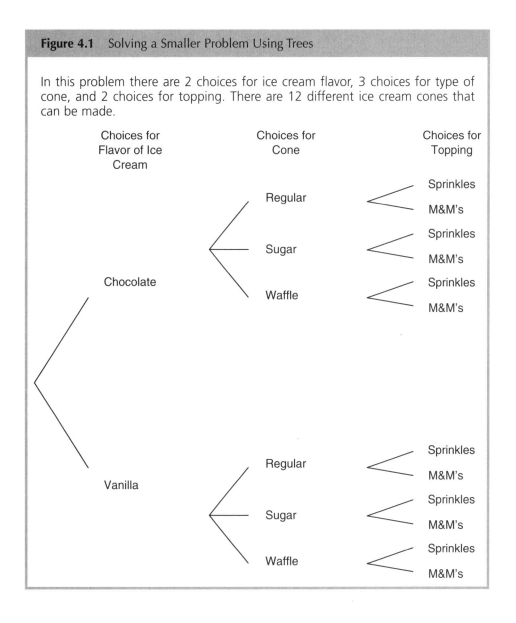

They also went over Question 3 on the homework. (How many different flavors, toppings, and cones would Mr. Garrett have to have to make the statement about the 500 different cones true? Identify at least two different ways of determining these figures.) Since this problem is open ended, the students arrive at a variety of appropriate answers depending on the number of scoops of ice cream, toppings, and cones they choose to offer the customers. There are so many different types of questions the students create that Mrs. Wilson could easily spend the entire class period having students present their different "cones." Some of the answers they provide follow.

For the single scoop with a single topping answer, the student's answers are fairly similar. Many students determine that 30 different flavors of ice cream have to be used to come up with over 500 different types of cones: Their solution is arrived at because 30 different flavors, 6 toppings, and 3 types of cones combine for 540 different single dip cones. For a double scoop (2 different flavors of ice cream and using the assumption that order matters) and single topping, the students are surprised that it takes so few flavors of ice cream with 6 kinds of toppings and 3 different types of cones to get over 500 different combinations. They find that their answer is 6 (flavors of ice cream) × 5 (flavors of ice cream) × 6 (toppings) × 3 (cones) = 540. Another group tried a triple scoop cone (3 different flavors), 2 kinds of toppings (again different and using the assumption that order matters), and 1 cone. They found that 4 × 3 × 2 × 6 × 5 × 3 = 2160. So Mr. Garrett would only have to have 4 kinds of ice cream, 6 different types of toppings, and 3 kinds of cones to make 2,160 different triple scoop cones! Consequently, the students decide that Mr. Garrett could make many more types of cones than he advertised based on the number of scoops (single, double, or triple), number of toppings, and type of cone. They are eager to report their findings to Mr. Garrett and the principal and will do so in the next few days.

Mrs. Wilson is happy that students are getting the feel for figuring out permutations without using the formula, which is complicated and tends to be difficult for students to understand. She knows that eventually students will encounter the formula, but she wanted to give them a firm understanding of what permutations really are. Her goal was to help them understand the concept of permutations without having to memorize or rely on the formulas. In the next day or two she decides she will continue with this topic, including combinations and other more challenging problems that build on the ice cream cone scenario.

DISCUSSION

This activity was designed to include a variety of learners in a variety of ways. You may have noticed that students are engaged in this activity in ways we discussed in Chapter 3. Each of the elements of the lesson contributes in a significant way toward addressing the affective, behavioral, and cognitive factors. Students were engaged affectively when the lesson was interesting and provided attainable levels of success so that they could develop a positive attitude toward learning mathematics. Students were engaged behaviorally by the interactive design of the activity, necessitating participation and communication. Finally, by working on challenging problems that have multiple solutions, students were required to develop strategies for attacking the problem situations, which speaks to the cognitive factor of engagement.

In these activities you may have noticed some of Glasser's Five Basic Needs being met among the students. Mrs. Wilson encouraged a *sense of belonging* in the classroom by integrating a mathematics lesson with the upcoming field day, in which they will all participate. She also fostered a sense of belonging by creating an atmosphere of learning where everyone could participate at some level and by acknowledging and encouraging students for their efforts. A sense of *freedom* was promoted by allowing students to make choices regarding their learning. In this case, students could choose their own problem-solving strategies as well as their methods to solve the problems. Since there were multiple solutions to some questions, students were allowed flexibility in their answers. *Power* (competence) was instilled by having students explain their understandings to the rest of the class and by acknowledging students' quality work. Finally, Mrs. Wilson added a *fun* element to her lesson by enabling students to be active in solving a meaningful problem relevant to their lives.

The design of this activity is also inclusive for special needs students. Research suggests that special needs students benefit from using appropriate methods to facilitate understanding of mathematical concepts. Students such as ELLs and low achievers have more opportunities for success in such an activity, because they can be cognitively engaged at an appropriate level. The activity includes elements from all three of Bruner's stages: the concrete, the pictorial, and the symbolic, thus providing elements of mathematics at several different levels.

SUMMARY

At this point, we hope you have begun to consider how your philosophy of teaching mathematics becomes intertwined with your philosophy of classroom engagement. Carefully planning your lessons to include the best practices from Chapter 1, ideas from the principles and standards in Chapter 2, and the key elements of engagement (affective, behavioral, and cognitive) discussed in Chapter 3 will provide you with tools to successfully engage your students in learning mathematics.

Again let us emphasize that engagement issues are intertwined. Although we have separated out the issues for discussion purposes and have even addressed certain pieces of the vignettes as affective, behavioral, or cognitive, each of these impacts the others. Because of this interrelatedness, it is important to focus on all three domains when teaching mathematics. As you focus on each of these domains in your teaching, you will begin to notice an increase in your students' engagement and knowledge of mathematics.

The following is a summary of engagement strategies to address the special populations we discussed in this chapter.

Summary of Strategies to Engage Special Populations

❖ Know your learner. Obtain a variety of information from different sources to help you best teach your student.

❖ Create a positive classroom culture. Set and expect high standards for achievement from all students.

❖ Increase opportunities for communication and participation.

❖ Differentiate instructional strategies.

---

5 Assessment

In this chapter we will discuss the following:

❖ Assessment

❖ Types of Assessment Tools

❖ Backward Design

❖ Data Driven Instructional Practices

Assessment is a key component in helping you teach all of your learners, a tool to help you determine whether your methods of instruction are successful. According to the National Council of Teachers of Mathematics (NCTM, 1995), there are four major purposes for assessment: (1) monitoring student progress, (2) making instructional decisions, (3) evaluating student achievement, and (4) evaluating programs. You can see that in addition to being used to evaluate students for grades, assessment can inform and shape lessons as it sheds light on what does and does not work for particular students. Keeping with the focus on diverse groups of learners, we present several different strategies for assessing understanding and for assessing special needs populations. As you read through this chapter, be sure to keep all learners in mind, including the ones you read about in Chapter 4.

> Assessment is a key component in helping you teach all of your learners, a tool to help you determine whether your methods of instruction are successful.

As you begin your teaching career, you must consider many aspects of assessment that will guide your philosophy of teaching. In this chapter we will discuss how to assess learners through different types of assessments and rubrics. We will illustrate these assessments using the activities from Chapters 1–4. Adaptations for special populations are also discussed.

TYPES OF ASSESSMENT

The NCTM (2000) describes several types of assessment, which range from traditional unit tests or quizzes to open-ended projects. Some of the assessments will be formative in nature; that is, the assessment provides information for monitoring the teaching and learning process. Formative assessments are used to help teachers determine next steps during the learning process. Other assessments will be summative assessments designed to gauge student understanding after a concept or unit has been taught. In this section, we develop an item representative of each of the different types of assessment.

Unit Tests and Quizzes

Most textbook publishers provide a number of supplemental materials to accompany mathematics textbooks, one of these being a collection of quizzes and unit tests that are aligned with the chapters of the book. Their usefulness varies, and you should take time to review them carefully to determine whether they assess what you wish to assess in the manner you wish to assess it. Tests involving many multiple-choice and short-answer items are easy to administer and to grade, but you need to consider what information you are gathering about the knowledge your students have been developing over the course of the unit. Assessments that are based on recall of facts and procedures are different from those based on students' ability to solve problems and knowledge of when to use relevant facts and procedures. You will want to strike a balance. As we have mentioned previously, Bloom's taxonomy is crucial to instruction; it is also important to assessment. Since you are trying to determine what a student knows about a topic through assessment, asking multiple levels of questions is important. We start with a typical multiple choice question that may be used to assess the concept of proportional reasoning learned after completing the Shake Across America activity:

It takes 2 seconds for 3 people to shake hands. How long does it take for 12 people to shake hands?

   a. 7 seconds   b. 14 seconds
   c. 8 seconds   d. 6 seconds

This assessment question may be used on quizzes, tests, or even home-work assignments. Unit tests and quizzes, whether written by you or obtained along with the textbook, serve a purpose in assessing students' knowledge. This multiple choice assessment item, however, belongs on the lower end of Bloom's taxonomy. It could be classified as a simple application of proportional reasoning. It does not assess higher-level thinking from Bloom's perspective. In order to gain a more complete picture of what your students understand, consider other forms of assessment and other levels on Bloom's taxonomy. We present a variety of options here.

Open-Middled and Open-Ended Questions

Open-middled questions are questions that students will be able to solve correctly in more than one way. True open-ended questions are questions with more than one correct answer. Open-middled questions are more common than open-ended questions. These types of questions require students to show their work, so that teachers can gain insight into their thinking. These questions allow the teacher to determine the strategies used by the students as well as the manner in which the students have carried out their chosen strategy.

An example of an open-middled question was provided in the Surface Area With Polydron Shapes vignette in Chapter 1. The question was the following:

> Given a square prism (a cube), how does the surface area of the prism change if each side dimension is doubled? Tripled? Quadrupled? Can you find any patterns in your answers?

Students demonstrated more than one way to approach this problem. One group approached the problem by building the prisms with the Polydron shapes, while another group drew the nets of the prisms on graph paper. When looking for patterns in the answers, some groups analyzed the size of the nets that they had drawn on graph paper; other groups organized their data in a table to look for patterns in the numbers. In all, students approached this problem concretely, visually, and numerically. Although most students in the vignette did not do this, this problem could also be approached algebraically, and students could find a function that generalizes their patterns. This problem illustrates the analysis level of Bloom's taxonomy, since students are being asked to look for patterns in their findings. This part of the lesson challenges students beyond simple understanding of procedures and rules; they must think more deeply about the concepts involved.

The Shake Across America activity in Chapter 1 is an example of an open-ended activity. It is open ended since there is a range of possible "correct" answers, and there is no one "correct" answer. In fact, the "correct" answer is not even known and would be different every time if the handshake across America were actually to occur in real life. The most important part about this activity is the mathematical reasoning used to get an answer, not the final answer itself.

Here are some other examples of open-ended assessments:

1. Estimate how long it will take for the "wave" to go all the way around Fenway Park during Game 7 of the World Series.

2. Determine how many books the total eighth grade student population at Fisher Middle School can read in a month.

Note that students will have to collect data to complete these open-ended assessments, and students will have to make decisions about how to analyze the data and incorporate their findings into their solution method. For this reason, every answer may be slightly different. At face value, these problems can be labeled as application problems according to Bloom's taxonomy. However, the act of collecting data pushes the level of the problem up into the analysis, synthesis, and evaluation ranges, since students have to make decisions about the worthiness of their data (whether any mistakes were made when collecting the data) and how to use their data to help them determine a solution to the problem. These last two problems may be used as homework assessments in their current form. If you want to assess understanding of the Shake Across America activity on a quiz or an exam, you could use the Fenway Park problem, but you would need to give students the circumference of Fenway Park along with sample data of how long a wave takes for three, six, and nine people. You could then ask students to determine how long the entire wave will take. The book problem could also be used on a quiz if you provide some data about the number of books different students at the school can read in a month.

Projects

The benefit for assigning a project is that it enables you to assess higher-level abilities. Problem-solving abilities in particular are difficult to assess in a 40-minute testing situation. Many really interesting problems cannot be solved in five minutes and require students to work on them over a period of several days or even weeks. Remember the classic book report that is assigned several weeks in advance, or the science fair project that may take a month or more to complete? Projects in mathematics should be thought of in the same light, as something that requires time to develop and to be completed over a period of time. The Shake Across America activity might be modified to be used as a miniproject when studying proportional reasoning and slope. For example, you might not give the distance across the United States, nor give them the directions as written in the assignment. You might just leave it open ended and have students construct their own ways of thinking about the project and complete it in that manner.

The carnival problem from Chapter 3 can also be used as a project. Recall that students were asked to use their understanding of probability to create carnival games that would generate money for the seniors. They were also asked to verify that their game actually generates money for the seniors and to justify their reasoning in creating the game. This is an excellent example of a project in which students use basic probability along with geometric probability to create two games—one involving two dice and one involving a dartboard. Students investigate the mathematics behind the carnival game, simulate the game, and verify, both theoretically and experimentally, that their games actually work. They may also be asked to create the backdrop for their games, with a list of the rules for the game, which can be used at the actual carnival.

Portfolios

A portfolio is a collection of work that students have completed over a period of time. This can include everything a student has done for an entire unit, including homework, tests, quizzes, and projects, or it may be a specific subset of those items. You may want to ask your students to include several pieces of work in their portfolios: the piece of work they are most proud of, the assignment they enjoyed doing the most, the one that needed the most revision, or one they worked on further than necessary (a type of extension). The goal for the students in creating a portfolio with specific items of their choosing is to be reflective about the work they have done. They should be encouraged to look at each piece of work with a critical eye and to reflect on the unit as a whole.

Journals

Another means of assessing student progress is through the use of journals. You may also want to use the journal as a means of gauging the affective climate of your classroom related to mathematics. Journals will tell you whether the frustration or satisfaction level is high on any given unit. By assigning prompts such as, "My favorite or least favorite part of this assignment was. . . ." you will be able to quickly tell what emotions your students are experiencing as they learn the mathematics.

You may also choose to use the journal as a way to dig deeper into the topic of the day or week. Thinking questions, such as, "Explain why you used ratios to solve this problem," or "Write down any patterns you noticed in this activity," will encourage students to think more deeply about the concepts presented to them. A journal item involving proportional reasoning and slope might look like this:

> Explain how you used the ideas of proportional reasoning and slope to predict how long the handshake across America would take. Why were your answers to each part different? Discuss the strengths and weaknesses of using each method (proportional reasoning and slope) to predict the amount of time the handshake would take.

> **You may also choose to use the journal as a way to dig deeper into the topic of the day or week.**

This journal incorporates analysis and synthesis as well as evaluation, which are the top levels of Bloom's taxonomy. Students are asked to analyze their solutions and to evaluate the use of each method.

Observation and Questioning

Classroom teachers are continually observing, interacting, and collecting information about their students. This information can be used for one or more of the four main purposes of assessment mentioned in the beginning of this chapter: (1) monitoring student progress, (2) making instructional decisions, (3) evaluating student achievement, and (4) evaluating programs. The use of observation and questioning can serve to help you decide what to do next in your instruction as well as inform your pacing and provide evidence for evaluation. Although observation and questioning are generally used by teachers informally, here are some suggestions on ways to formalize what you do naturally as you teach.

Simply documenting your observations and interactions will transform your class time into usable information for assessment. The documentation method you choose will depend on your purposes of assessment. Informal assessment for the purpose of monitoring student progress and making instructional decisions can be documented in a notebook in free form as the observations occur.

An observational checklist to be filled out daily can be as detailed or as minimal as necessary for the students involved. For example, the teacher may keep detailed notes about how much time a student has been on task during the class period or merely use a checklist as simple as this one:

Name: _____

Date: _____

_____ did/did not participate fully in class today

_____ did/did not complete class work

Notes:

Other instruments, such as the following one that uses a 4-point scale, can be used to evaluate student progress in cooperative learning activities:

Name: _____

The student contributed appropriately to the group project. 1   2   3   4

The student worked collaboratively.   1   2   3   4

Concepts and skills the student learned in this project:

Concepts and skills the student still does not understand:

NOTE: 1 is the lowest; 4 is the highest

This tool may be used to determine whether the goals of instruction were met and whether the students are ready to progress to the next topic.

More formal assessments—such as evaluating student performance on a particular problem or set of problems—may take the form of a specific set of questions related to the mathematics in the given problem. For example, if you are assigning grades to the open-ended questions on proportional reasoning and slope described in the previous section, and you want to ask students questions about their work as part of their grade, you will probably include specific questions, such as these:

❖ Describe your method for finding the answer using a ratio.
❖ How do you know that you can use the slope to determine the answers?
❖ What patterns did you notice during the solution process?

Observations and questioning can be invaluable tools in both formal and informal assessments used to make on-the-spot changes in a lesson plan or for the next day and coming weeks. As we discussed, this does not need to be a time-intensive or paper-intensive process. Careful preplanning to organize the exact information desired will make the process easier. For further ideas on assessment, see the NCTM's practical handbooks for mathematics assessment (NCTM, 1999, 2000).

> Observations and questioning can be invaluable tools in both formal and informal assessments used to make on-the-spot changes in a lesson plan or for the next day and coming weeks.

RUBRICS

Rubrics are tools to assess problems that require students to explain their thinking and show their work. Rubrics allow the teacher to look at the final product in a holistic manner, focusing on the overall correctness of the solution. An example follows of a holistic rubric for grade levels 6 through 12.

Rubric to Assess Learning	
Points	*Description of Work Required*
4	Solution is correct with complete work shown. The student explains the thought process completely, and appropriate use of diagrams and/or pictures or models is utilized.
3	Solution is generally complete but with minor errors. Errors may include explanations that cannot be followed, procedural mistakes, or absence or incorrect use of pictures or diagrams.
2	Solution is partially complete; however, not enough work is shown to determine how the student arrived at the solution. There are substantial errors in reasoning or computation.
1	Work shown has flaws in computation or logic. The answer may also be incorrect.
0	No response.

Again, think back to the assignment Mr. Edwards gave his students and to one solution for the dice game discussed in Chapter 3:

Proposal for the Seniors or "House" Winning and Thus Making Money
It will cost $1 to play the game for one roll of the two dice. If you get an even product, you lose the $1 you paid to play; if you get an odd product, you win a small stuffed animal (costing 50 cents).

Students justified this game in the following manner. If 200 people play the game, then you will initially make $200. Since $\frac{3}{4}$ of the outcomes are even, $\frac{3}{4} \times 200$, or 150, people would be expected to lose. Since $\frac{1}{4}$ of the outcomes are odd, $\frac{1}{4} \times 200$, or 50, people would be expected to win a small stuffed animal. Fifty stuffed animals will cost $50 \times (.50) = \$25$, so the total amount the seniors would expect to make for 200 students playing the game will be about $175. A table was included to demonstrate the experimental results of their game being played on a graphing calculator.

Using this response as an example, and the rubric to assess learning above, a teacher may assign a value of 4 to this answer, since the answer is correct and the work was thorough and presented in complete sentences.

Another possible student solution for the dice game given in Chapter 3 (this one is for a fair game) is the following:

It will cost $1 to play the game for one roll of the two dice. If you get an even sum of the two dice, you win $1, and if you get an odd sum with the two dice, you lose $1.

This response would be given a 2, since the solution is partially complete, and students have made some progress on the problem. The problem has not been well thought out, however, and there are some flaws in the reasoning (discussed in Chapter 3). There is also a lack of justification.

DEVELOPING ASSESSMENTS: THE USE OF BACKWARD DESIGN

All too often, assessment is the last thing considered when planning a lesson. The teacher plans the lesson, teaches it, and then, often as an afterthought, decides on an assessment, picking out problems that seem to address the main ideas or simply using the assessments supplied with the book. The use of backward design ensures that assessment is among the first things a teacher considers when designing a lesson. According to Wiggins and McTighe (1998),

Rather than creating assessments near the conclusion of a unit of study (or relying on the tests provided by textbook publishers, which may not completely or appropriately assess our standards), backward design calls for us to operationalize our goals or our standards in terms of assessment evidence as we begin to plan a unit or a course. (p. 8)

Backward design forces teachers to think about how they are going to assess what they want students to know before they begin instruction, which often clarifies the goals for instruction.

Stages of Backward Design

There are three stages involved in the process of backward design. After each is discussed, an example is provided to help you understand the simplicity and necessity for this process in assessment.

Stage 1: Identify Desired Results

The first step is to determine the standards (district, state, and/or NCTM) that you will address for the lesson or unit. Then consider the topics, skills, and resources that need to be examined. Next, important knowledge (such as facts, concepts, and principles) as well as skills (processes, strategies, and methods) should be considered. Finally, look at the enduring understandings that anchor the unit—the big ideas. All of these big ideas should be delineated at this time.

For example, if you want to focus on the major goal of developing number sense, you must first select the standards that you wish to address. Let's look at one of NCTM's standards for number and operations in Grades 6–8: "Understand numbers, ways of representing numbers, relationships among numbers, and number systems." Students should be able to work flexibly with fractions, decimals, and percentages to solve problems; to compare and order fractions, decimals, and percentages efficiently; and to find their approximate locations on a number line. Students should also be able to work with fractions, decimals, and percentages in a problem-solving scenario. For example, students can be asked to determine the percentage of students who are reading at the eighth grade level if two-fifths of the 256 students are reading at the eighth grade level. Students should be able to give their answer in terms of a percentage despite the question being stated in terms of a fraction.

Stage 2: Determine Acceptable Evidence

The big question that we consider here is, "How will you determine whether your students have achieved the desired results?" Wiggins and

McTighe (1998) suggest a variety of assessment methods that include informal checks for understanding, observations and dialogue, quizzes and tests, open-ended prompts, and performance tasks and projects. The most important piece at this stage is to determine the methods you will use to assess your students.

Using the standard for numbers and operations for Grades 6–8 that we looked at in Stage 1, we can think about how to assess understanding throughout the instructional activities. One example could be to provide students with a group of fractions, decimals, and percentages and ask them to order them from least to greatest, noting any that are equivalent and explaining their reasoning.

Stage 3: Plan Learning Experiences

Once you have determined the desired outcomes and created or selected appropriate ways for learning to be assessed, you are now ready to plan instructional activities. For example, an activity that may be used to facilitate student understanding is using either Cuisenaire rods or pattern blocks to have students create representations of fractions; this method may also be used to show relative size and to compare one fraction to another. Another activity, using decimal squares, may be used to compare sizes of decimals and to show their relationship to percentages.

GRADING AND ASSESSMENT SCHEMES

As you continue to develop your philosophy on assessment, your grading schemes may evolve from one year to the next. In the beginning, many mathematics teachers are inclined to use more traditional testing as a means to assess their learners. However, as time goes by and they obtain more experience with the curriculum, they often begin to see a variety of ways in which student knowledge may be assessed.

One thing we would like you to consider in developing your grading scheme is the many ways that understanding can be demonstrated. For example, your special needs students or English language learners may perform better in nontraditional assessment tasks, such as projects and other open-ended assignments. This is not to say you should eliminate a formal end-of-chapter exam, but you might want to consider other means of obtaining the same information using a variety of modalities. Some teachers base their entire end-of-quarter or semester grade on just chapter exams and quizzes. Others include individual and group projects, class presentations, and homework, in addition to tests and quizzes. Providing alternative opportunities to express knowledge will better inform you of your students' understanding and abilities.

PRACTICAL WAYS OF ASSESSING THROUGHOUT THE INSTRUCTIONAL PROCESS

Let us reiterate this important point: Assessment can take many forms and should not be limited to formal quizzes, tests, or projects. Remember, assessment is important to inform instruction, and there are multiple opportunities for assessment throughout the instructional process. For example, an informal assessment may take place as you are providing a warm-up problem at the beginning of the class. As the students work on the problem, walk around and observe how they are progressing, the strategies they are using, and any difficulties they may be encountering. These informal observations may be recorded in a variety of ways. You can mentally take note of the observations, keep written notes in free form, or use a formal checklist to record your findings. Any assigned work can also be used as a formal or informal assessment. You can also assess your students through questioning techniques, preplanned activities, and any techniques used to wrap up the day's activities.

> Assessment can take many forms and should not be limited to formal quizzes, tests, or projects.

Of course, formal assessments may also be used, such as tests, projects, and quizzes. You might not use each of these types of assessments every day or even every week. However, over the course of an entire unit, you can include quite a few of the different types. You may even want to look at varying your assessments over the course of an entire grading period or even over an entire year. For example, you may include one project per grading period, one journal entry per week, a summative evaluation at the end of the year, and so forth. As you become more comfortable with your teaching, you will more easily focus on what the students are saying and doing in order to craft your instruction.

TAILORING ASSESSMENTS FOR SPECIAL POPULATIONS

To appropriately assess your special learners, it is essential to consider their individual needs. Does the student have motor difficulties so that written work is larger than normal or writing is laborious? Does the student have visual processing difficulties that cause him or her to sometimes combine the information from one problem with that of the next? Or is the student an English language learner? All of these needs should be considered, as should the goals for the assessment, before you create or adapt an existing assessment for a student. All of the assessments we have discussed in this chapter may be modified according to your students' needs in order to obtain information about their mathematical understandings.

Figure 5.1 is an example of an exam prior to modifications made for students with disabilities, and Figure 5.2 is the answer sheet for students to use with it. Figure 5.3 provides a look at an edited portion of this exam. It demonstrates one possible way to make a test easier to read. Two of the

(Text continues on page 96)

Figure 5.1   Exam Before Modifications

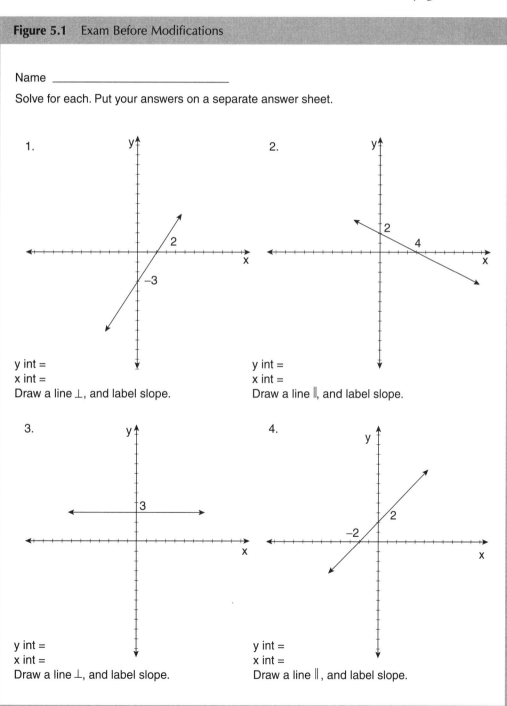

Name _____

Solve for each. Put your answers on a separate answer sheet.

1.

2

−3

y int =
x int =
Draw a line ⊥, and label slope.

2.

2

4

y int =
x int =
Draw a line ∥, and label slope.

3.

3

y int =
x int =
Draw a line ⊥, and label slope.

4.

2

−2

y int =
x int =
Draw a line ∥, and label slope.

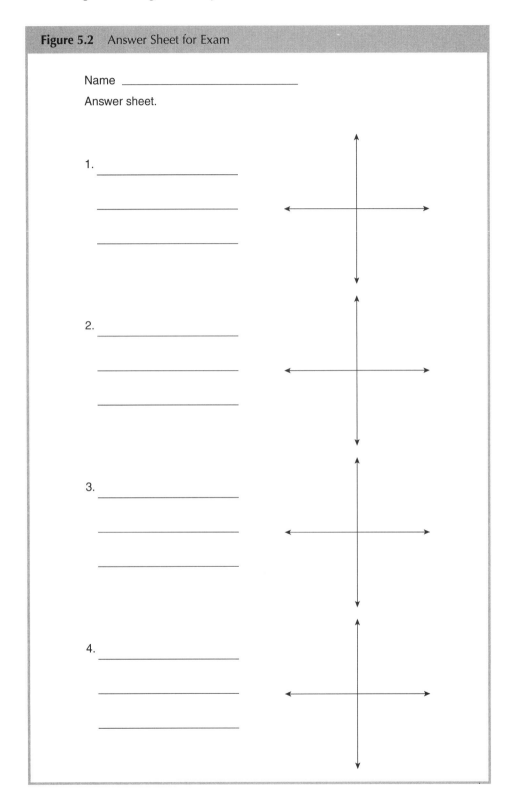

Figure 5.2 Answer Sheet for Exam

Figure 5.3 Exam With Modifications Made for Special Needs

Name _____

Solve each problem completely. Read the directions for each problem.

1. Find the y intercept and the x intercept for the line graphed.

   y intercept = _____ x intercept = _____

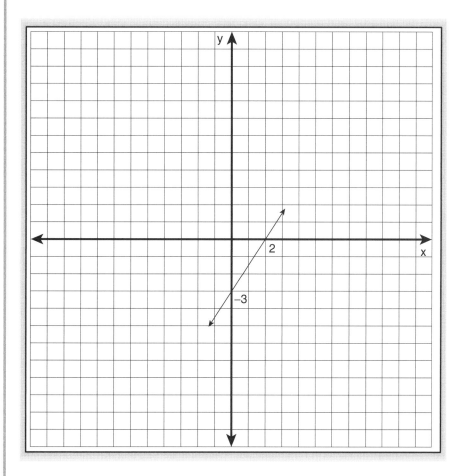

Graph a line that is perpendicular to the one that is graphed above and label its slope.

Slope of the line = _____

(Continued)

Figure 5.3 (Continued)

2. Find the y intercept and the x intercept for the line graphed.

y intercept = _____   x intercept = _____

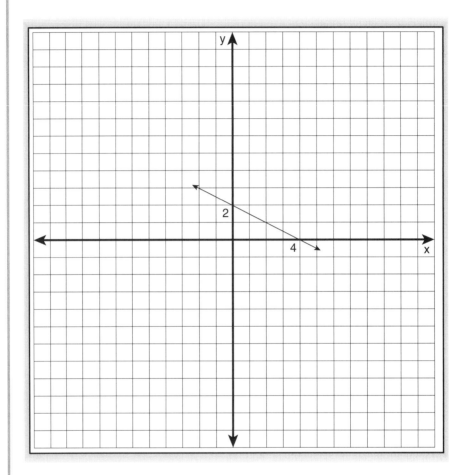

Graph a line that is parallel to the one that is graphed above and label its slope.

Slope of the line = _____

(Text continued from page 93)

four problems are shown; extra space is provided for each, and each problem is typed and the text is set off to alleviate confusion among problems. There are reminders for each problem to show work, draw a picture, and write the answer in a complete sentence. The directions are written very clearly, and there are fewer problems per page. In addition, the required information needed for each problem is written out for each one. It may be necessary to include one or two problems per page, depending on the student. Students write their answers on the test sheet; there is no separate answer sheet. All of these modifications create fewer distractions for the student, hopefully allowing for more success.

DATA DRIVEN INSTRUCTIONAL PRACTICES

Recently, data analysis and the meetings involved with it have become an integral part of many teachers' weekly schedules. Previously, data analysis was primarily left to administrators, who traditionally collected the data from state- or district-given tests and provided the analysis for the teachers after the school year had ended. This process has shifted in many schools so that the information gathered may be used to impact instruction immediately. This shift has also included using various forms of assessment, not just high-stakes testing assessments. The goal is to increase student achievement by tailoring instruction on the basis of data collected. Meetings to discuss data can take on a variety of forms depending on the faculty makeup, data collection techniques, and methods of analysis. Typically, teachers meet to discuss a specific course and content. For example, sixth grade teachers at one school may decide to create a common assessment tool to assess student understanding of proportional reasoning. They may meet the following week with their students' test scores to discuss the results.

The discussion of these results is generally aimed at answering questions such as these:

1. Did the students master the material taught?

2. Were there any specific concepts or skills that the students did not master?

3. What were the instructional strategies used to instruct those skills or concepts? Were they appropriate?

4. If any remediation is needed, how and when will it be provided?

5. What are the next steps for instruction?

The questions addressed at such a meeting may vary, depending on the needs of the faculty. Generally, the goals are to inspect the data, determine remediation steps if necessary, and then plan for the next instructional steps. These meetings may be mandated at many schools or may be set up informally by groups of teachers to help them better tailor instruction to meet their students' needs.

A WORD ABOUT STANDARDIZED TESTS

Assessments fall into two major categories: criterion referenced and norm referenced. In most schools, classroom assessments that are administered by the classroom teacher are criterion-referenced assessments. According to FairTest: The National Center for Fair and Open Testing (n.d.), "Criterion-referenced tests are intended to measure how well a person has learned a specific body of knowledge and skills" (¶ 1). This is in contrast to norm-referenced tests. Many of the norm-referenced major exams that students take are commonly called standardized tests. The Scholastic Aptitude Test (SAT) is one example of a norm-referenced exam. A student's score depends on the performance of others who have taken the same assessment. Scores are placed along the normal distribution (bell-shaped curve), and then students are given a score relative to others' standings. In short, in a criterion-referenced assessment, students are judged relative to a predetermined performance standard or criterion. In a norm-referenced assessment, students are judged relative to the performance of other students taking the test.

SUMMARY

Assessment is a topic that is often left to the end of lesson planning and then not given the time it deserves. A main focus of this chapter is on careful consideration of the assessments you use with your students, both the types of assessments and the level of the questions asked. The discussion of different types of assessments should guide you in adapting commercially made assessments to meet your different evaluation needs. Keeping Bloom's taxonomy in mind when you choose assessments will help you to include problems at each of the different levels and will help you to tailor questions to elicit higher-order reasoning. The use of the backward design method discussed in this chapter will help you to gear your instruction to the desired outcomes rather than try to find an appropriate assessment instrument after the fact.

Now that we have addressed many of the big ideas involved in teaching mathematics, let us take some time to consider how all of these ideas fit together. That is the topic of the final chapter.

6 Putting It All Together

In this chapter we will discuss the following:

❖ Designing Your Curriculum
❖ Making Connections

Now that you have read about many of the important elements that make up a successful mathematics class, it's time to think about how it all fits together. In this chapter, we discuss ways for you to incorporate the core themes of this book throughout your mathematics curriculum. We show you how to connect big ideas within mathematics, and we present ideas for you to connect mathematics across the grades.

THE YEAR AT A GLANCE: DESIGNING YOUR CURRICULUM

One of the most crucial components of teaching is being well versed in your content area. Your education has provided experiences for you to grow in your understanding of the mathematics content you will be teaching in middle and high school. When creating your curriculum you will use that content knowledge, in addition to making decisions about what topics will be presented, how you will present the topics, and how long you will spend on each one. This process is often referred to as a scope and sequence. Well before you begin your first day of class, you will spend countless hours behind the scenes determining each element of your scope and sequence.

One important distinction to be aware of is that a mathematics text is not a curriculum; it is just a text. A curriculum is much more. Although each teacher at your grade level in your school will be using the same book, the way in which each of you chooses to implement the ideas in the text may be very different. It is the group of mathematical experiences, together with materials, that make up a curriculum.

> One important distinction to be aware of is that a mathematics curriculum is much more than the text you are using.

To begin, you should have a framework from which to pull your curriculum. As we discussed in Chapter 2, there are standards documents that explicitly describe the content that students should learn at each grade level. These documents, along with any school or district standards, are an excellent foundation from which to begin the development of your curriculum. Next, materials should be gathered that may be used to teach mathematics throughout the year. When developing a scope and sequence, it is most helpful if you can work with another individual who is experienced at teaching the specific content or age group, or if you have been given a scope and sequence on which to model your own.

A syllabus for your course may also need to be created. A syllabus forms part of the overall curriculum and usually includes the standards to be addressed, a suggested time line of instruction, and a grading scheme. Other teachers in your school who have taught this content and age group may have a syllabus that you can use as a guide to create your own.

Once you have developed your scope and sequence, this does not mean that you cannot deviate from the plan. Each year your students will arrive with different needs and abilities, based on their different mathematics backgrounds. For example, you may find you need to review linear functions when you thought you could just move on to quadratic functions; this could change your time line and alter your curriculum. As time progresses, you will gain a greater understanding of the students you are teaching at your age range as well as the content to be taught.

MAKING CONNECTIONS WITHIN MATHEMATICS

It may seem like a lot to ask teachers to cover all of the mandated standards as well as each section in the book. Indeed, many new (and not so new) teachers become overwhelmed trying to teach everything in the standards for their course. It may help to look at mathematics more holistically, instead of focusing on each lesson as a separate entity. If you view mathematics as a connected body of knowledge instead of a disjointed set of rules and ideas, it will be easier to adequately cover all of the standards. This is the concept behind the NCTM Curriculum Focal Points mentioned in Chapter 2. One approach is to incorporate activities into your instruction that address more than one standard at a time, such as the activities in the vignettes in previous chapters.

Connections Between Ratio and Slope

Let's take the time now to review the concepts incorporated into some of the previous activities in this book. Implicit in the Shake Across America activity is the connection between ratios and the slope of a linear function. During the activity, Mrs. Malloy makes this connection explicit. A lesson such as this one using real-world problems can be a great way for students to gain more experience with the concepts and skills underlying these topics. Although you may not initially teach ratio and slope at the same time, you can encourage a deeper understanding of both concepts by integrating them into a single activity.

Geometry and Algebra

Geometry and algebra are two areas of mathematics that are generally covered in separate courses, yet there are many natural opportunities to reinforce one while teaching the other. In the Surface Area With Polydron Shapes activity, the concept of area of two-dimensional figures was used to develop understanding of the surface area of three-dimensional figures. Geometric and algebraic reasoning were also intertwined when the investigation turned toward finding algebraic patterns of the changing surface areas as the result of increased dimensions. Often geometric patterns can be investigated in terms of their algebraic generalizations; fractals is one topic of study in mathematics that is rich in both geometric and algebraic patterns. On the flip side, when teaching linear functions in algebra, you can also incorporate geometric patterns to aid in generalization.

> When developing your curriculum, search for activities that address more than one concept at once.

These ideas are rich in that they involve more than one mathematical concept and demonstrate the connectedness of mathematical ideas. Whether you are introducing one concept or reinforcing the other concepts, this approach will allow you to address more than one item on your seemingly endless list of standards. When developing your curriculum, search for activities that address more than one concept at once. This should be one of your criteria when deciding whether or not to include a particular activity in your lessons.

MATHEMATICAL CONNECTIONS ACROSS THE GRADES

Within your classroom, you have many opportunities to connect the mathematics you are teaching to mathematics content that has already been taught or will be taught. These opportunities are within your reach, and it is wise to consider what other teachers have done with your students before, and what they will do with your students after you have taught them for a year. Mathematics is often taught in a spiraling manner, revisiting topics each year and building on previous knowledge to further understanding of each concept. When talking with your students' previous teachers, consider both touching base informally in an ongoing manner and connecting formally to determine the depth of knowledge your students reached in previous courses. This will go a long way toward ensuring that students receive the appropriate amount and level of instruction.

The Pizza Problem below is one example of an activity that connects content across the grades within a single activity. This problem can be challenging for a middle school student on one level as well as a high school senior or first year college student taking calculus, on a completely different level.

The Pizza Problem

Your father sneaks into the kitchen one night and eats half of an entire pizza that he finds on the counter. On the second day he comes back and eats half of what remains of the pizza from the first day; on the third day he comes in and eats half of what remains from the second day. If your father continues this process for seven days, how much of the pizza has he eaten? How much is left?

What is the pattern? Is the sum approaching a number?

Draw a picture, explain the pattern you see, and defend your reasoning.

This problem is inspired by a version of the classic Zeno's Paradox problem involving a race between a tortoise and Achilles (Zeno's paradox, n.d.). The beauty of this problem is that it addresses an amazing amount of mathematics at many different levels, and you can take it as far as your students are ready and willing to go. The versatility of this problem is that it can be approached at a very concrete level, using manipulatives and/or pictures, and it can be addressed at an abstract level using geometric series and limits. This problem also involves many of the NCTM process standards: problem solving, reasoning and proof, connections, and multiple representations, and it can also include communication.

Let's take a look at the problem at a middle school level, using pictures, fractions, and decimals.

Middle School Students

Middle school students can draw pictures of the pizza and divide it into halves, fourths, eighths, and so on. If needed, students can use circle fraction pieces as manipulatives to assist them in their investigations. Students can keep track of the amount of pizza eaten and the amount left using fractions or decimals. Their work can be organized in a table in order to discover patterns that can be generalized (see Figure 6.1).

Students can observe the pattern that the amount left keeps decreasing by one half and gets closer and closer to zero. In addition, the amount eaten gets closer to one, which would be the entire pizza. Informal ideas of limit can be introduced by asking students the question, "Will your father ever eat the entire pizza?"

Algebra

Students can be asked to find the functions that represent the amount of the pizza eaten and amount remaining. Both functions are exponential functions, with the amount left being $\left(\frac{1}{2}\right)^n$ and the amount eaten being

$$\frac{(2^n - 1)}{2^n}.$$

Students can investigate these functions graphically and determine that the horizontal asymptotes are $y = 0$ and $y = 1$, respectively.

Precalculus and Calculus

Delving deeper into the analysis of this problem, students can be asked to explore the following questions:

❖ What is the nth term of the sequence?
❖ What is the sum of the n terms of the sequence? What is the limit of this function as n approaches infinity?

Figure 6.1 Amount of Pizza Eaten in Pizza Problem

Number of Days	Amount Eaten Each Day	Image	Total Amount Eaten	Total Amount Eaten in Decimals	Total Amount Left
1	$\frac{1}{2}$	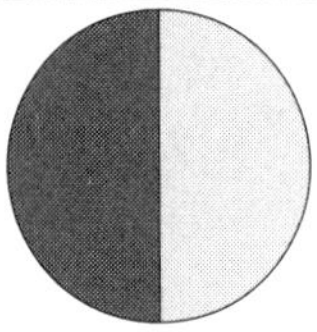	$\frac{1}{2}$	.5	$\frac{1}{2}$
2	$\frac{1}{4}$	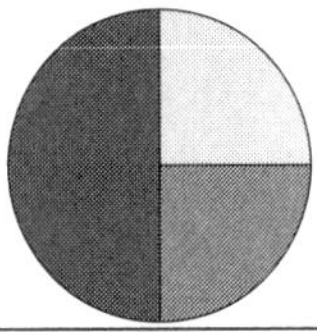	$\frac{3}{4}$	.75	$\frac{1}{4}$
3	$\frac{1}{8}$	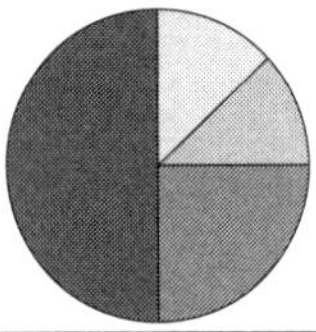	$\frac{7}{8}$	.875	$\frac{1}{8}$
4	$\frac{1}{16}$	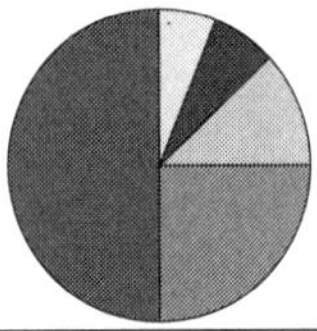	$\frac{15}{16}$	.9375	$\frac{1}{16}$
5	$\frac{1}{32}$	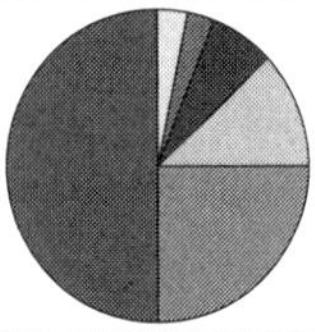	$\frac{31}{32}$	.969	$\frac{1}{32}$
6	$\frac{1}{64}$	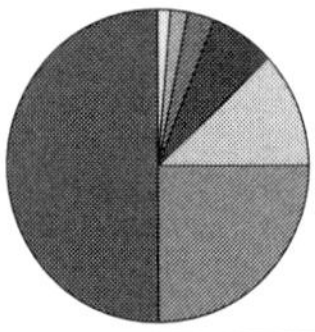	$\frac{63}{64}$	.984	$\frac{1}{64}$
7	$\frac{1}{128}$	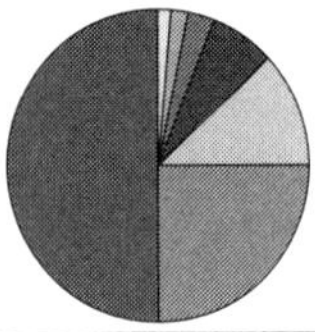	$\frac{127}{128}$	.992	$\frac{1}{128}$
n	$\frac{1}{2^n}$		$1 - \frac{1}{2^n}$ or $\frac{2^n - 1}{2^n}$	Approaches 1	$\frac{1}{2^n}$ (Approaches 0)

These students can investigate the amount eaten as a sum of a geo-metric series. For example, on Day 1, the amount eaten is $\frac{1}{2}$; on Day 2 it is $\frac{1}{2}+\frac{1}{4}$; on Day 3 it is $\frac{1}{2}+\frac{1}{4}+\frac{1}{8}$. This sum is a geometric series $\Sigma\left(\frac{1}{2}\right)^k$, where k ranges from 1 to n. This geometric series has a closed form for the sum of the first n terms as well as a closed form for the sum as n goes to infinity.

Extensions

The following extensions can be addressed at an appropriate level for each of the Grades 6–12. (See Appendix D for details on these adaptations and extensions.)

Extension 1: What if your father came and ate only $\frac{1}{3}$ of the pizza the first night, then on the second night he ate $\frac{1}{3}$ of what he had eaten on the first night (or $\frac{1}{9}$ of the entire pizza), then on day 3 he ate $\frac{1}{3}$ of what he had eaten on day 2 (or $\frac{1}{27}$ of the entire pizza). How much of the pizza would he have eaten after seven days? What is the pattern?

Extension 2: Repeat this problem for powers of $\frac{1}{4}$, powers of $\frac{1}{5}$, and so forth. What patterns do you notice?

Students will notice that when your father eats $\frac{1}{3}, \frac{1}{9}, \frac{1}{27}$, and so forth, the limit of what he eats is $\frac{1}{2}$. When he eats $\frac{1}{4}, \frac{1}{16}, \frac{1}{64}$, and so forth, the limit of what he eats is $\frac{1}{3}$. They can also determine that the total amount eaten is

$$\left(\frac{1}{(a-1)}\right),$$

where $\frac{1}{a}$ is the amount eaten on the first night.

MORE CONNECTIONS ACROSS THE GRADES

Another important consideration in making connections across the grades is the manner in which a certain topic has been taught. One of the problems inherent in our teacher credentialing system is that elementary and secondary level teachers often have few opportunities to learn how mathematics is taught at a different level. Further, due to the logistics of the school building placement, many teachers have few opportunities to collaborate with teachers at other levels to find out how they are teaching mathematics. It is one thing to walk down the hall to ask the calculus teacher how he or she approaches the idea of limits so that you can use a similar method in your precalculus class. It is quite another issue, however, to contact a teacher from one of your feeder elementary schools to discuss how their school introduces the concept of area so that you can build on this understanding when you teach area in geometry.

Your school district may have opportunities for you to participate in discussions on teaching mathematics across grade levels. If so, we would encourage you to participate in those discussions. Not only will you learn a great deal about how elementary teachers present mathematics, you can begin to make connections to what they are doing and what you are doing at the secondary level. As well, it may help you conceptually teach the content when you see how far back in skills and concepts you may have to go to reach all of your students. If your school does not offer such opportunities, then this book is a good starting point for learning about some of the ways that connections can be made across the grade levels.

For example, algebra can be thought of as generalized arithmetic. Manipulatives used to teach multiplication, the base ten blocks, are generalized to become algebra tiles for teaching algebraic manipulations. The distributive property that students use naturally in elementary school to figure out multiplication facts that they don't know (e.g., 9×12 becomes 9×10 plus 9×2) is formalized in an algebra course. Middle and high school teachers can capitalize on student understandings from elementary school by building on prior knowledge and sense making with manipulatives used in lower grades.

A common activity in elementary school related to area involves using a grid to determine the area of an irregular shape (the child's hand, for example). Students can get more refined estimates by using progressively smaller grids. This activity becomes formalized when finding the area under the curve using trapezoids with progressively smaller widths in a calculus course.

MAKING CONNECTIONS ACROSS THE CURRICULUM

A common goal of many math educators is to cultivate students who are able to apply their understanding of mathematics in their lives outside of math class. One way to encourage such mathematical literacy in students is to address mathematical reasoning as it occurs in other courses and in life events. Here we use two examples to describe how to integrate other content areas into the teaching of secondary mathematics.

Shake Across America Revisited

The Shake Across America activity from Chapter 1 can be expanded into a cross-curricular project. After showing one of the many YouTube videos of the Hands Across America event in the 1980s, you can talk about the motivation behind the original event, which lends itself well to discussion of social issues related to economics as well as charity events. Connections can be made between the efforts that were made in the 1980s and what is being done today. Students can investigate statistics on the income levels in the United States and the number of people who qualify for government aid in some form. (Amanda McKee, personal communication, December, 2008). They could be asked to produce scatter plots for each year and to find the change from year to year. This change from year to year would introduce the concept of slope, setting the stage for the activity outlined in Chapter 1.

Election Years Activity

Another idea for a cross-curricular project draws on current events during an election year. There are numerous ways to use mathematics when discussing the likelihood of different candidates being elected president. The use of statistics is prevalent in predicting the outcome of any race. Students can learn about the statistics involved in the election polling and projection process. They can then conduct their own poll in their school or town to determine public opinion on candidates.

Students can also use mathematics to determine the various combinations of states necessary to win the election. By knowing the number of electoral votes each state has and how many are needed to win the presidency, students can create various scenarios for different ways each candidate could possibly win the election. The use of results from election polling, as well as knowledge of which states historically support a particular party and which are key swing states, can be incorporated to make this a rich, ongoing activity.

We have given you a couple of ideas for incorporating real-life situations into your curriculum. Keep your eye out for others as you continue to create your lesson plans for the year.

SUCCEEDING AT TEACHING MATHEMATICS—AND LOVING IT!

In this book, we have provided you with some food for thought on the many intricacies involved in teaching and learning mathematics. Ultimately, you need to be convinced that what you are doing in the classroom is the best for your students' mathematical development. Try out the ideas and principles from this book so that you can begin to determine how you can make them best work for you and become part of your overall teaching philosophy.

As a new teacher of mathematics, you will go a long distance toward professional confidence and significantly impact the way your students perform in your mathematics class if you start the year well. Very often, new teachers concentrate so hard on all the details that they lose sight of the big picture. A major message of this book is to keep the big ideas in mathematics, as well as your students, front and center. Focus on the main concepts in each of the courses you are teaching. Make explicit the connections to other mathematics they have already learned, and connect their prior learning to new material using methods that are familiar to them as well. You, as the teacher, realize that math is a connected body of knowledge and not just a disjoint collection of rules and procedures. Provide rich learning experiences for your students so that they can come to realize this as well. By paying close attention to the big ideas in mathematics and the various ways your students learn, the details will fall into place, and you can help all students reach their highest potential in mathematics.

> A major message of this book is to keep the big ideas in mathematics, as well as your students, front and center.

We hope that after reading this book you feel more prepared to take on the challenges that teachers of mathematics continually face. Although each day may not be perfect, we hope that you do not lose sight of your goals and your reasons for choosing this profession in the first place. Although this book is focused on ways to engage students in learning the big ideas in mathematics, do your best to make sure that you are engaged in the teaching process as well. It is a journey that you embark on with your students and, as important as it is for the students to enjoy the journey, it is just as important for you to enjoy what you have worked so hard to create.

Appendix A

Solutions to Shake Across America

Sample Data Collected for Problems 1–3

Number of People	Distance (feet)	Time 1 (seconds)	Time 2 (seconds)	Average Time
3	6	2.4	2.8	2.6
6	12	6.1	5.9	6.0
9	18	9.3	9.7	9.5
12	24	12.8	11.9	12.35

Answers to Proportional Reasoning Section

Distance (feet)	Average Time	Feet/Second	Seconds/Foot
6	2.6	2.3	.43
12	6.0	2.0	.5
18	9.5	1.89	.53
24	12.35	1.94	.51
Average		2.03	.49

4. $\dfrac{People}{Foot} = \dfrac{1}{2}$

5. $\dfrac{1}{2} = \dfrac{x}{15,000,000} \Rightarrow x = 7,500,000$ people

6. 2 ft/sec; .5 sec/ft

7. $\dfrac{5 \text{ sec}}{1 \text{ ft}} = \dfrac{x}{15,000,000} \Rightarrow x = 7,500,000 \text{ sec} = 86.8$ days

8. A proportion (two equivalent ratios of seconds to feet) is used to determine the total amount of time it takes for the handshake to travel across America.

Algebraic Reasoning

9. Plot will have the following points:

Distance (X values)	Average Time (Y values)
6	2.6
12	6.0
18	9.5
24	12.35

10. $f(x) = .55x - .575$ (found by using linear regression on a graphing calculator)

11. Slope is the rate of change in sec/ft; in part A (#6 above), our ratio was $\approx .5$

12. The y-intercept should be 0 in theory, since a distance of 0 feet should take 0 seconds to travel.

13. f(15,000,000) = 8,187,499 sec = 94.8 days

Appendix B

*Solution to the Following
Problem From the Polydron Vignette*

G iven a square prism (a cube), how does the surface area of the prism change if each side dimension is doubled? Tripled? Quadrupled? Can you find any patterns in your answers?

Rectangular Prisms

Length	Width	Height	Surface Area	Algebraic Pattern
1	1	1	6	$6(1)^2$
2	2	2	24	$6(2)^2$
3	3	3	54	$6(3)^2$
4	4	4	96	$6(4)^2$
n	n	n	$6(n)^2$	$6(n)^2$

When the dimensions are doubled, the surface area is four times the original area. When the dimensions are tripled, the surface area is nine times the original area. In general, if you multiply the dimensions of the cube by n, the surface area is multiplied by n^2.

Appendix C

The Dart Board Game Solution

This game can be a winning game for the carnival depending on what the seniors decide to charge the students to play the game. Let's analyze what the expected value should be.

I. Find the area of the circular regions:

Area of circle with radius $1 = \pi$ square inches

The area of the middle "ring" with radius 3 can be found by first finding the area of the circle with the radius 3 and then subtracting out the area of the center circle with radius 1.

The following details this calculation:

Area of the circle with radius of $3 = 9\pi$ square inches

Area of circle with radius of $1 = 1\pi$ square inches

Area of the ring $= 9\pi - 1\pi = 8\pi$ square inches

To find the area of the larger ring, determine the area for the larger circle with radius of 5 (25π), and subtract out the area of the circle with radius of 3 (9π). This will give you 16π square inches.

II. Find the expected value (or average payout):

Expected value =

($10) (probability of hitting the center of the circle)

+ ($5) (probability of hitting the area in the middle of the circle)

+ ($1) (probability of hitting the area of the outer circle)

$$= (10)(\pi / 25\pi) + (5)(8\pi / 25\pi) + (1)(16\pi / 25\pi)$$

$$= .40 + 1.60 + .64$$

$$= \$ 2.64$$

That means that this game would be a losing game for the school if they charged less than $ 2.64.

If the seniors charged each person at least $2.64 to play the game, they would make a profit. For example if they charged $3, then the seniors would theoretically make $0.36 per student who played. If 200 students played the game, then the total revenue for this game would be (200)(.36) = $72. If the seniors decided to charge $4, then the school would theoretically make $1.36 per student who played. If 200 students played the game, the total revenue would be (200)(1.36) = $272.

Appendix D

Generalization for Original Pizza Problem

Number of Days	Amount Eaten per Day	Total Amount Eaten	Total Amount Eaten in Decimals	Total Amount Left
n	$\dfrac{1}{2^n}$	$1-\dfrac{1}{2^n}$ or $\dfrac{2^n-1}{2^n}$	Approaches 1	$\dfrac{1}{2^n}$ (Approaches 0)

Solution to Extension 1

Number of Days	Amount Eaten per Day	Total Amount Eaten	Total Amount Eaten in Decimals	Total Amount Left
1	$\dfrac{1}{3}$	$\dfrac{1}{3}$	.333	$\dfrac{2}{3}=.667$
2	$\dfrac{1}{9}$	$\dfrac{1}{3}+\dfrac{1}{9}$	.444	$\dfrac{5}{9}=.556$
3	$\dfrac{1}{27}$	$\dfrac{1}{3}+\dfrac{1}{9}+\dfrac{1}{27}=\dfrac{13}{27}$	.481	$\dfrac{14}{27}=.519$
4	$\dfrac{1}{81}$	$\dfrac{40}{81}$	.494	$\dfrac{41}{81}=.506$
5	$\dfrac{1}{243}$	$\dfrac{121}{243}$	.498	$\dfrac{122}{243}=.502$

(Continued)

(Continued)

Number of Days	Amount Eaten per Day	Total Amount Eaten	Total Amount Eaten in Decimals	Total Amount Left
6	$\dfrac{1}{729}$	$\dfrac{364}{729}$	.499	$\dfrac{365}{729} = .500$
7	$\dfrac{1}{2187}$	$\dfrac{1092}{2187}$	.4998	$\dfrac{1095}{2187} = .500$
n	$\dfrac{1}{3^n}$	$\dfrac{\frac{1}{2}\left(3^n - 1\right)}{3^n}$	Approaches $\dfrac{1}{2}$	$1 - \dfrac{\frac{1}{2}\left(3^n - 1\right)}{3^n}$ Approaches $\dfrac{1}{2}$

In the total amount eaten, the numerator is a little less than half the denominator. To get the numerator, subtract 1 from the denominator and divide by 2.

Solution to Extension 2

The amount eaten for powers of $\frac{1}{4}$ is

$$\frac{\frac{1}{3}(4^n - 1)}{4^n}.$$

It approaches $\frac{1}{3}$ of the whole pizza.

In general, for powers of $\frac{1}{a}$, the amount eaten is

$$\left[\frac{1}{(a-1)}\right]\frac{(a^n - 1)}{a^n}.$$

This value will approach $\frac{1}{(a-1)}$ as n approaches infinity.

References

Anderson, L., & Krathwohl, D. (Eds.). (2001). *A taxonomy for learning, teaching, and assessing: A revision of bloom's taxonomy.* New York: Addison Wesley Longman.

Baxter, J. A., Woodward, J., & Olson, D. (2001). Effects of reform-based mathematics instruction on low achievers in five third-grade classrooms. *The Elementary School Journal, 101*(5), 529–547.

Bresser, R. (2003). Helping English-language learners develop computational fluency. *Teaching Children Mathematics, 9,* 294–299.

Brown, H. D. (2001). *Teaching by principles: An interactive approach to language pedagogy* (2nd ed.). White Plains, NY: Longman.

Bruner, J. (1966). *Toward a theory of instruction.* Cambridge, MA: Harvard University Press.

Charles, R. I., Dossey, J. A., Leinwand, S. J., Seeley, C. L., & Vonder Embse, C. B. (1998). *Middle school math, course 2.* Menlo Park, CA: Scott Foresman–Addison Wesley.

Collier, V. P. (1989). How long? A synthesis of research on academic achievement in a second language. *TESOL Quarterly, 23,* 509–531.

FairTest: The National Center for Fair & Open Testing. (n.d.). *Criterion- and standards-reference tests.* Retrieved April 23, 2007 from http://www.fairtest.org/facts/csrtests.html

Gay, G. (2000). *Culturally responsive teaching: Theory, research, & practice.* New York: Teachers College Press.

Glasser, W. (1998). *Choice theory: A new psychology of personal freedom.* New York: Harper Collins.

Grouws, D. A., & Cebulla, K. J. (2000). *Improving student achievement in mathematics: Part 1. Research findings.* Columbus, OH: ERIC Clearinghouse for Science, Mathematics, and Environmental Education. (ERIC Document Reproduction Service No. ED463952).

Hartman, B., & Tarone, E. (1999). Preparation for college writing: Teachers talk about writing instruction for Southeast Asian American students in secondary school. In L. Harklau, K. Losey, & M. Siegal (Eds.), *Generation 1.5 meets college composition* (pp. 99–118). Mahwah, NJ: Lawrence Erlbaum.

Hiebert, J., & Carpenter, T. (1992). Learning and teaching with understanding. In D. A. Grouws (Ed.), *Handbook of research on mathematics teaching and learning* (pp. 65–97). New York: Macmillan.

Hogan, B., & Forsten, C. (2007). *8-step model drawing.* Peterborough, NH: Crystal Springs Books.

Johnson, D. T. (1993). Mathematics curriculum for the gifted. In J. Van TasselBaska (Ed.), *Comprehensive curriculum for gifted learners* (2nd ed., pp. 231–261). Boston: Allyn & Bacon.

Johnson, D. T. (2000). *Teaching mathematics to gifted students in a mixed-ability classroom*. Reston, VA: Council for Exceptional Children.

LaCelle-Peterson, M., & Rivera, C. (1994). Is it real for all kids? A framework for equitable assessment policies for English language learners. *Harvard Educational Review, 64*(1), 55–75.

Maccini, P., & Hughes, C. A. (2000). Effects of a problem solving strategy on the introductory algebra performance of secondary students with learning disabilities. *Learning Disabilities Research and Practice, 15*, 10–21.

Maker, C. J. (1982). *Curriculum development for the gifted*. Rockville, MD: Aspen.

Matthews, L. E. (2005). Towards design of clarifying equity messages in mathematics reform. *The High School Journal, 88*(4), 46–58.

Mercer, C. D., & Mercer, A. R. (1998). *Teaching students with learning problems* (5th ed.). Upper Saddle River, NJ: Prentice Hall/Merrill.

Montague, M. (1997). Student perception, mathematical problem solving, and learning disabilities. *Remedial and Special Education, 18*(1), 46–53.

Mullis, I. V. S., Martin, M. O., & Foy, P. (with Olson, J. F., Preuschoff, C., Erberber, E., Arora, A., & Galia, J.). (2008). *TIMSS 2007 international mathematics report: Findings from IEA's trends in international mathematics and science study at the fourth and eighth grades*. Chestnut Hill, MA: TIMSS & PIRLS International Study Center, Boston College.

National Association for Gifted Children. (2005). *Socio-emotional guidance and counseling: Exploring guiding principle 4*. Retrieved April 23, 2007, from http://www.nagc.org/index.aspx?id=458

National Council of Teachers of Mathematics. (1989). *Curriculum and evaluation standards for school mathematics*. Reston, VA: Author.

National Council of Teachers of Mathematics. (1991). *Professional standards for teaching mathematics*. Reston, VA: Author.

National Council of Teachers of Mathematics. (1995). *Assessment standards for school mathematics*. Reston, VA: Author.

National Council of Teachers of Mathematics. (1999). *Mathematics assessment: A practical handbook for grades 9–12*. Reston, VA: Author.

National Council of Teachers of Mathematics. (2000). *Mathematics assessment: A practical handbook for grades 6–8*. Reston, VA: Author.

National Council of Teachers of Mathematics. (2000). *Principles and standards for school mathematics*. Reston, VA: Author.

National Council of Teachers of Mathematics. (2006). *Curriculum focal points for prekindergarten through grade 8 mathematics: A quest for coherence*. Reston, VA: Author.

National Mathematics Advisory Panel. (2008). *Foundations for success: The national mathematics advisory panel final report 2008*. Washington DC: U.S. Department of Education.

Pintrich, P. R., & Schrauben, B. (1992). Students' motivational beliefs and their cognitive engagement in classroom academic tasks. In D. H. Schunk & J. Meece (Eds.), *Student perceptions in the classroom* (pp. 149–179). Hillsdale, NJ: Lawrence Erlbaum.

Polya, G. (1945). *How to solve it!* Garden City, NY: Doubleday.

Sliva, J. A. (2003). *Teaching inclusive mathematics to special learners, K–6.* Thousand Oaks, CA: Corwin.

Sliva, J. A., & Roddick, C. (2001). Mathematics autobiographies: A window into beliefs, values, and past mathematics experiences of preservice teachers. *Academic Education Quarterly, 5*(2), 101–107.

Tucson Unified School District. (n.d.). *Best practices in teaching mathematics.* Tucson Unified School District Balanced Literacy Booklets, High School. Retrieved April 23, 2007, from http://instech.tusd.k12.az.us/balancedlit/handbook/BLHS/blmathhs.htm

Wiggins, G., & McTighe, J. (1998). *Understanding by design.* Alexandria, VA: Association for Supervision and Curriculum Development.

Zeno's paradox of the tortoise and Achilles. (n.d.). In *Platonic realms interactive mathematics encyclopedia.* Retrieved October 29, 2009, from http://www.mathacademy.com/pr/prime/articles/zeno_tort/index.asp

Index

CORWIN
A SAGE Company

The Corwin logo—a raven striding across an open book—represents the union of courage and learning. Corwin is committed to improving education for all learners by publishing books and other professional development resources for those serving the field of PreK–12 education. By providing practical, hands-on materials, Corwin continues to carry out the promise of its motto: **"Helping Educators Do Their Work Better."**